IELTS

GENERAL TRAINING 15

WITH ANSWERS

AUTHENTIC PRACTICE TESTS

Cambridge University Press
www.cambridge.org/elt

Cambridge Assessment English
www.cambridgeenglish.org

Information on this title: www.cambridge.org/9781108781626

© Cambridge University Press and Cambridge Assessment 2020

First published 2020

20 19 18 17 16 15 14 13 12 11 10 9 8 7 6 5 4 3 2 1

Printed in Malaysia by Vivar Printing

A catalogue record for this publication is available from the British Library

ISBN 978-1-108-78161-9 Academic Student's Book with Answers with Audio
ISBN 978-1-108-78162-6 General Training Student's Book with Answers with Audio

Contents

Introduction

Prepare for the exam with practice tests from Cambridge

Inside you'll find four authentic examination papers from Cambridge Assessment English. They are the perfect way to practise – EXACTLY like the real exam.

Why are they unique?

All our authentic practice tests go through the same design process as the IELTS test. We check every single part of our practice tests with real students under exam conditions, to make sure we give you the most authentic experience possible.

Students can practise these tests on their own or with the help of a teacher to familiarise themselves with the exam format, understand the scoring system and practise exam technique.

Further information

IELTS is jointly managed by the British Council, IDP: IELTS Australia and Cambridge Assessment English. Further information can be found on the IELTS official website at: **ielts.org**.

WHAT IS THE TEST FORMAT?

IELTS consists of four components. All candidates take the same Listening and Speaking tests. There is a choice of Reading and Writing tests according to whether a candidate is taking the Academic or General Training module.

Academic	**General Training**
For candidates wishing to study at undergraduate or postgraduate levels, and for those seeking professional registration.	For candidates wishing to migrate to an English-speaking country (Australia, Canada, New Zealand, UK), and for those wishing to train or study below degree level.

The test components are taken in the following order:

Listening		
4 parts, 40 items, approximately 30 minutes		
Academic Reading	or	**General Training Reading**
3 sections, 40 items		3 sections, 40 items
60 minutes		60 minutes
Academic Writing	or	**General Training Writing**
2 tasks		2 tasks
60 minutes		60 minutes
Speaking		
11 to 14 minutes		
Total Test Time		
2 hours 44 minutes		

GENERAL TRAINING TEST FORMAT

Listening

This test consists of four parts, each with ten questions. The first two parts are concerned with social needs. The first part is a conversation between two speakers and the second part is a monologue. The final two parts are concerned with situations related to educational or training contexts. The third part is a conversation between up to four people and the fourth part is a monologue.

A variety of question types is used, including: multiple choice, matching, plan/map/ diagram labelling, form completion, note completion, table completion, flow-chart completion, summary completion, sentence completion and short-answer questions.

Candidates hear the recording once only and answer the questions as they listen. Ten minutes are allowed at the end for candidates to transfer their answers to the answer sheet.

Reading

This test consists of three sections with 40 questions. The texts are taken from notices, advertisements, leaflets, newspapers, instruction manuals, books and magazines. The first section contains texts relevant to basic linguistic survival in English, with tasks mainly concerned with providing factual information. The second section focuses on the work context and involves texts of more complex language. The third section involves reading more extended texts, with a more complex structure, but with the emphasis on descriptive and instructive rather than argumentative texts.

A variety of question types is used, including: multiple choice, identifying information (True/False/Not Given), identifying the writer's views/claims (Yes/No/Not Given), matching information, matching headings, matching features, matching sentence endings, sentence completion, summary completion, note completion, table completion, flow-chart completion, diagram-label completion and short-answer questions.

Writing

This test consists of two tasks. It is suggested that candidates spend about 20 minutes on Task 1, which requires them to write at least 150 words, and 40 minutes on Task 2, which requires them to write at least 250 words. Task 2 contributes twice as much as Task 1 to the Writing score.

In Task 1, candidates are asked to respond to a given situation with a letter requesting information or explaining the situation. They are assessed on their ability to engage in personal correspondence, elicit and provide general factual information, express needs, wants, likes and dislikes, express opinions, complaints, etc.

In Task 2, candidates are presented with a point of view, argument or problem. They are assessed on their ability to provide general factual information, outline a problem and present a solution, present and justify an opinion, and to evaluate and challenge ideas, evidence or arguments.

Candidates are also assessed on their ability to write in an appropriate style. More information on assessing the Writing test, including Writing assessment criteria (public version), is available at ielts.org.

Speaking

This test takes between 11 and 14 minutes and is conducted by a trained examiner. There are three parts:

Part 1

The candidate and the examiner introduce themselves. Candidates then answer general questions about themselves, their home/family, their job/studies, their interests and a wide range of similar familiar topic areas. This part lasts between four and five minutes.

Part 2

The candidate is given a task card with prompts and is asked to talk on a particular topic. The candidate has one minute to prepare and they can make some notes if they wish, before speaking for between one and two minutes. The examiner then asks one or two questions on the same topic.

Part 3

The examiner and the candidate engage in a discussion of more abstract issues which are thematically linked to the topic in Part 2. The discussion lasts between four and five minutes.

The Speaking test assesses whether candidates can communicate effectively in English. The assessment takes into account Fluency and Coherence, Lexical Resource, Grammatical Range and Accuracy, and Pronunciation. More information on assessing the Speaking test, including Speaking assessment criteria (public version), is available at ielts.org.

HOW IS IELTS SCORED?

IELTS results are reported on a nine-band scale. In addition to the score for overall language ability, IELTS provides a score in the form of a profile for each of the four skills (Listening, Reading, Writing and Speaking). These scores are also reported on a nine-band scale. All scores are recorded on the Test Report Form along with details of the candidate's nationality, first language and date of birth. Each Overall Band Score corresponds to a descriptive statement which gives a summary of the English-language ability of a candidate classified at that level. The nine bands and their descriptive statements are as follows:

9 **Expert User** – *Has fully operational command of the language: appropriate, accurate and fluent with complete understanding.*

8 **Very Good User** – *Has fully operational command of the language with only occasional unsystematic inaccuracies and inappropriacies. Misunderstandings may occur in unfamiliar situations. Handles complex detailed argumentation well.*

7 **Good User** – *Has operational command of the language, though with occasional inaccuracies, inappropriacies and misunderstandings in some situations. Generally handles complex language well and understands detailed reasoning.*

6 **Competent User** – *Has generally effective command of the language despite some inaccuracies, inappropriacies and misunderstandings. Can use and understand fairly complex language, particularly in familiar situations.*

5 **Modest User** – *Has partial command of the language, coping with overall meaning in most situations, though is likely to make many mistakes. Should be able to handle basic communication in own field.*

4 **Limited User** – *Basic competence is limited to familiar situations. Has frequent problems in understanding and expression. Is not able to use complex language.*

3 **Extremely Limited User** – *Conveys and understands only general meaning in very familiar situations. Frequent breakdowns in communication occur.*

2 **Intermittent User** – *No real communication is possible except for the most basic information using isolated words or short formulae in familiar situations and to meet immediate needs. Has great difficulty understanding spoken and written English.*

1 **Non User** – *Essentially has no ability to use the language beyond possibly a few isolated words.*

0 **Did not attempt the test** – *No assessable information provided.*

MARKING THE PRACTICE TESTS

Listening and Reading

The answer keys are on pages 121–128.
Each question in the Listening and Reading tests is worth one mark.

Questions which require letter / Roman numeral answers

- For questions where the answers are letters or Roman numerals, you should write *only* the number of answers required. For example, if the answer is a single letter or numeral you should write only one answer. If you have written more letters or numerals than are required, the answer must be marked wrong.

Questions which require answers in the form of words or numbers

- Answers may be written in upper or lower case.
- Words in brackets are *optional* – they are correct, but not necessary.
- Alternative answers are separated by a slash (/).
- If you are asked to write an answer using a certain number of words and/or (a) number(s), you will be penalised if you exceed this. For example, if a question specifies an answer using NO MORE THAN THREE WORDS and the correct answer is 'black leather coat', the answer 'coat of black leather' is *incorrect*.
- In questions where you are expected to complete a gap, you should only transfer the necessary missing word(s) onto the answer sheet. For example, to complete 'in the …', where the correct answer is 'morning', the answer 'in the morning' would be *incorrect*.
- All answers require correct spelling (including words in brackets).
- Both US and UK spelling are acceptable and are included in the answer key.
- All standard alternatives for numbers, dates and currencies are acceptable.
- All standard abbreviations are acceptable.
- You will find additional notes about individual answers in the answer key.

Writing

The sample answers are on pages 129–136. It is not possible for you to give yourself a mark for the Writing tasks. We have provided sample answers (written by candidates), showing their score and the examiners' comments. These sample answers will give you an insight into what is required for the Writing test.

HOW SHOULD YOU INTERPRET YOUR SCORES?

At the end of each Listening and Reading answer key you will find a chart which will help you assess whether, on the basis of your Practice Test results, you are ready to take the IELTS test.

In interpreting your score, there are a number of points you should bear in mind. Your performance in the real IELTS test will be reported in two ways: there will be a Band Score from 1 to 9 for each of the components and an Overall Band Score from 1 to 9, which is the average of your scores in the four components. However, institutions considering your application are advised to look at both the Overall Band Score and the Band Score for each component in order to determine whether you have the language skills needed for a particular course of study or work environment. For example, if you are applying for a course which involves a lot of reading and writing, but no lectures, listening skills might be less important and a score of 5 in Listening might be acceptable if the Overall Band Score was 7. However, for a course which has lots of lectures and spoken instructions, a score of 5 in Listening might be unacceptable even though the Overall Band Score was 7.

Once you have marked your tests, you should have some idea of whether your listening and reading skills are good enough for you to try the IELTS test. If you did well enough in one component, but not in others, you will have to decide for yourself whether you are ready to take the test.

The Practice Tests have been checked to ensure that they are the same level of difficulty as the real IELTS test. However, we cannot guarantee that your score in the Practice Tests will be reflected in the real IELTS test. The Practice Tests can only give you an idea of your possible future performance and it is ultimately up to you to make decisions based on your score.

Different institutions accept different IELTS scores for different types of courses. We have based our recommendations on the average scores which the majority of institutions accept. The institution to which you are applying may, of course, require a higher or lower score than most other institutions.

Test 1

PART 1   *Questions 1–10*

Complete the notes below.

*Write **ONE WORD AND/OR A NUMBER** for each answer.*

Listening test audio

Bankside Recruitment Agency

- Address of agency: 497 Eastside, Docklands
- Name of agent: Becky **1** ....
- Phone number: 07866 510333
- Best to call her in the **2** ....

Typical jobs

- Clerical and admin roles, mainly in the finance industry
- Must have good **3** .... skills
- Jobs are usually for at least one **4** ....
- Pay is usually **5** £ .... per hour

Registration process

- Wear a **6** .... to the interview
- Must bring your **7** .... to the interview
- They will ask questions about each applicant's **8** ....

Advantages of using an agency

- The **9** .... you receive at interview will benefit you
- Will get access to vacancies which are not advertised
- Less **10** .... is involved in applying for jobs

PART 2   *Questions 11–20*

Questions 11–14

*Choose the correct letter, **A**, **B** or **C**.*

Listening test audio

Matthews Island Holidays

11   According to the speaker, the company

   A   has been in business for longer than most of its competitors.
   B   arranges holidays to more destinations than its competitors.
   C   has more customers than its competitors.

12   Where can customers meet the tour manager before travelling to the Isle of Man?

   A   Liverpool
   B   Heysham
   C   Luton

13   How many lunches are included in the price of the holiday?

   A   three
   B   four
   C   five

14   Customers have to pay extra for

   A   guaranteeing themselves a larger room.
   B   booking at short notice.
   C   transferring to another date.

Questions 15–20

Complete the table below.

Write **ONE WORD AND/OR A NUMBER** *for each answer.*

Timetable for Isle of Man holiday		
	Activity	**Notes**
Day 1	Arrive	Introduction by manager Hotel dining room has view of the **15** ....
Day 2	Tynwald Exhibition and Peel	Tynwald may have been founded in **16** .... not 979.
Day 3	Trip to Snaefell	Travel along promenade in a tram; train to Laxey; train to the **17** .... of Snaefell
Day 4	Free day	Company provides a **18** .... for local transport and heritage sites.
Day 5	Take the **19** .... railway train from Douglas to Port Erin	Free time, then coach to Castletown – former **20** .... has old castle.
Day 6	Leave	Leave the island by ferry or plane

PART 3   *Questions 21–30*

Questions 21–26

What did findings of previous research claim about the personality traits a child is likely to have because of their position in the family?

Listening test audio

*Choose **SIX** answers from the box and write the correct letter, **A–H**, next to Questions 21–26.*

Personality Traits
A   outgoing
B   selfish
C   independent
D   attention-seeking
E   introverted
F   co-operative
G   caring
H   competitive

Position in family

21   the eldest child   ....

22   a middle child   ....

23   the youngest child   ....

24   a twin   ....

25   an only child   ....

26   a child with much older siblings   ....

Questions 27 and 28

*Choose the correct letter, **A**, **B** or **C**.*

27 What do the speakers say about the evidence relating to birth order and academic success?

    A   There is conflicting evidence about whether oldest children perform best in intelligence tests.

    B   There is little doubt that birth order has less influence on academic achievement than socio-economic status.

    C   Some studies have neglected to include important factors such as family size.

28 What does Ruth think is surprising about the difference in oldest children's academic performance?

    A   It is mainly thanks to their roles as teachers for their younger siblings.

    B   The advantages they have only lead to a slightly higher level of achievement.

    C   The extra parental attention they receive at a young age makes little difference.

Questions 29 and 30

*Choose **TWO** letters, **A–E**.*

Which **TWO** experiences of sibling rivalry do the speakers agree has been valuable for them?

    A   learning to share

    B   learning to stand up for oneself

    C   learning to be a good loser

    D   learning to be tolerant

    E   learning to say sorry

PART 4   *Questions 31–40*

Complete the notes below.

*Write **ONE WORD ONLY** for each answer.*

Listening test audio

The Eucalyptus Tree in Australia

Importance

- it provides **31** .... and food for a wide range of species
- its leaves provide **32** .... which is used to make a disinfectant

Reasons for present decline in number

A) Diseases

(i)   'Mundulla Yellows'
- Cause – lime used for making **33** .... was absorbed
- – trees were unable to take in necessary iron through their roots

(ii) 'Bell-miner Associated Die-back'
- Cause – **34** .... feed on eucalyptus leaves
- – they secrete a substance containing sugar
- – bell-miner birds are attracted by this and keep away other species

B) Bushfires

William Jackson's theory:
- high-frequency bushfires have impact on vegetation, resulting in the growth of **35** ....
- mid-frequency bushfires result in the growth of eucalyptus forests, because they:

  – make more **36** .... available to the trees

  – maintain the quality of the **37** ....
- low-frequency bushfires result in the growth of **38** '.............................. rainforest', which is:

  – a **39** .... ecosystem

  – an ideal environment for the **40** .... of the bell-miner

---

READING

SECTION 1   *Questions 1–14*

Read the text below and answer Questions 1–6.

Consumer advice

What to do if something you ordered hasn't arrived

If something you've ordered hasn't arrived, you should contact the seller to find out where it is. It's their legal responsibility to make sure the item is delivered to you. They should chase the delivery company and let you know what's happened to your item. If your item wasn't delivered to the location you agreed (e.g. if it was left with your neighbour without your consent), it's the seller's legal responsibility to sort out the issue.

If the item doesn't turn up, you're legally entitled to a replacement or refund. You can ask for your money back if you don't receive the item within 30 days of buying it. If the seller refuses, you should put your complaint in writing. If that doesn't work, you could contact their trade association – look on their website for this information, or contact them to ask.

You might also be able to get your money back through your bank or payment provider – this depends on how you paid.

- If you paid by debit card, contact your bank and say you want to use the 'chargeback' scheme. If the bank agrees, they can ask the seller's bank to refund the money to your account. Many bank staff don't know about the scheme, so you might need to speak to a supervisor or manager. You should do this within 120 days of when you paid.
- If you paid by credit card and the item cost less than £100, you should contact your credit card company and say you want to use the 'chargeback' scheme. There's no time limit for when you need to do this. If the item cost more than £100 but less than £30,000, contact your credit card company and say that you want to make a 'section 75' claim.
- If you paid using PayPal, use PayPal's online resolution centre to report your dispute. You must do this within 180 days of paying.

Questions 1–6

Do the following statements agree with the information given in the text on page 16?

In boxes 1–6 on your answer sheet, write

> **TRUE**   *if the statement agrees with the information*
> **FALSE**   *if the statement contradicts the information*
> **NOT GIVEN**   *if there is no information on this*

1   You will receive a card telling you if an item has been left with a neighbour.

2   It may be quicker to get a refund than a replacement for a non-delivered item.

3   You are entitled to a refund if the item fails to arrive by a certain time.

4   There is a time limit when using the 'chargeback' scheme for a debit card payment.

5   You can use the 'chargeback' scheme for a credit card payment of more than £100.

6   PayPal's online resolution centre has a good reputation for efficiency.

Read the text below and answer Questions 7–14.

Rice cookers

What's the best rice cooker for you?

A   Ezy Rice Cooker

This has a 1.8 litre pot and a stainless steel exterior. It has a separate glass lid, and the handle on the lid stays cool. It produces perfectly cooked white rice, but tends to spit when cooking brown rice. There are slight dirt traps around the rim of the lid, and neither the pot nor the lid is dishwasher safe.

B   Family Rice Cooker

This has a plastic exterior and a flip-top lid. The lid locks when closed and becomes a secure handle to carry the cooker. The aluminium interior pot is quite difficult to clean, and it can't be put in a dishwasher. It's programmed to adjust the temperature once the rice is done so that it stops cooking but doesn't get cold.

C   Mini Rice Cooker

This has a flip-top lid and a 0.3 litre capacity. The interior pot is made of non-stick aluminium and is dishwasher safe. This rice cooker is ideal when cooking for one. However it does not have any handles at the side, and water sometimes overflows when cooking brown rice.

D   VPN Rice Cooker

This has a painted steel exterior with a handle on each side and a steel inner pot. It has a lift-off lid and comes with a booklet including a range of ideas for rice dishes. However, the keep-warm setting must be manually selected and the handles are tricky to grip.

E   S16 Rice cooker

This is simple to use, not spitting or boiling over even when cooking brown rice. The exterior stays cool when in use, so there's no danger of burning your hand. However, the lack of handles is a nuisance, and a recipe book would have been useful.

Questions 7–14

*Look at the five reviews of rice cookers, **A–E**, on page 18.*

For which rice cooker are the following statements true?

*Write the correct letter, **A–E**, in boxes 7–14 on your answer sheet.*

NB *You may use any letter more than once.*

7 The handles at the side are hard to use.

8 It cooks brown rice without making a mess.

9 It automatically switches setting to keep the rice warm when cooked.

10 It's difficult to get the removable top really clean.

11 A selection of recipes is provided with the cooker.

12 It has a handle at the top for carrying the cooker safely.

13 The outside of the cooker doesn't get too hot.

14 You can put the pot in the dishwasher.

→ ◳ p. 122

SECTION 2   *Questions 15–27*

Read the text below and answer Questions 15–22.

Safety when working on roofs

A fall from height is the most serious hazard associated with roof work. Preventing falls from roofs is a priority for *WorkSafe New Zealand*. Investigations by *WorkSafe* into falls that occur while working at height show that more than 50 percent of falls are from under three metres, and most of these are from ladders and roofs. The cost of these falls is estimated to be $24 million a year – to say nothing of the human costs that result from these falls. More injuries happen on residential building sites than any other workplace in the construction sector.

In order to prevent such injuries, a hazard assessment should be carried out for all work on roofs to assess potential dangers. It is essential that the hazards are identified before the work starts, and that the necessary equipment, appropriate precautions and systems of work are provided and implemented. Hazard identification should be repeated periodically or when there is a change in conditions, for example, the weather or numbers of staff onsite.

The first thing to be considered is whether it is possible to eliminate this hazard completely, so that workers are not exposed to the danger of falling. This can sometimes be done at the design, construction planning, and tendering stage. If the possibility of a fall cannot be eliminated, some form of edge protection should be used to prevent workers from falling. It may be possible to use the existing scaffolding as edge protection. If this is not practicable, then temporary work platforms should be used. In cases where such protection is not possible, then steps should be taken to minimise the likelihood of any harm resulting. This means considering the use of safety nets and other similar systems to make it less likely that injury will be caused if a fall does occur.

Ladders should only be employed for short-duration maintenance work such as touching up paint. People using ladders should be trained and instructed in the selection and safe use of ladders. There should be inspection of all ladders on a regular basis to ensure they are safe to use.

Questions 15–22

Complete the notes below.

*Choose **NO MORE THAN THREE WORDS AND/OR A NUMBER** from the text for each answer.*

Write your answers in boxes 15–22 on your answer sheet.

Safety when working on roofs

Investigations show that

- over half of falls are from less than **15** ....
- most falls are from ladders and roofs
- falls cost $24 million per year
- the majority of falls occur on **16** ....

Hazard identification should be carried out

- before the work starts
- when conditions such as the weather or worker numbers change

Controls

- **17** .... the hazard at the planning stage before the work begins if possible
- prevent a fall by using edge protection, e.g. scaffolding or **18** ....
- reduce the likelihood of injury, e.g. by using **19** ....

Ladders

- these should only be used for **20** .... which does not take a long time
- training should be provided in their **21** .... and use
- regular **22** .... of ladders is required

Read the text below and answer Questions 23–27.

Maternity Allowance for working women

You can claim Maternity Allowance once you've been pregnant for 26 weeks. Payments start 11 weeks before the date on which your baby is due.

The amount you can get depends on your eligibility. You could get either:
- £140.98 a week or 90% of your average weekly earnings (whichever is less) for 39 weeks
- £27 a week for 14 weeks

Maternity Allowance for 39 weeks

You might get Maternity Allowance for 39 weeks if one of the following applies:
- you're employed
- you're self-employed and pay Class 2 National Insurance (including voluntary National Insurance)
- you've recently stopped working

You may still qualify even if you've recently stopped working. It doesn't matter if you had different jobs, or periods when you were unemployed.

Maternity Allowance for 14 weeks

You might get Maternity Allowance for 14 weeks if for at least 26 weeks in the 66 weeks before your baby is due:
- you were married or in a civil partnership
- you were not employed or self-employed
- you took part in the business of your self-employed spouse or civil partner

How to claim

You'll need an MA1 claim form, available online. You can print this and fill it in, or fill it in online. You also need to provide a payslip or a Certificate of Small Earnings Exemption as proof of your income, and proof of the baby's due date, such as a doctor's letter.

You should get a decision on your claim within 24 working days.

You should report any changes to your circumstances, for example, if you go back to work, to your local Jobcentre Plus as they can affect how much allowance you get.

Questions 23–27

Complete the sentences below.

Choose NO MORE THAN TWO WORDS AND/OR A NUMBER from the text for each answer.

Write your answers in boxes 23–27 on your answer sheet.

23   The maximum amount of money a woman can get each week is
     £ ....

24   Being .... for a time does not necessarily mean that a woman
     will not be eligible for Maternity Allowance.

25   In order to claim, a woman must send a .... or a Small
     Earnings Exemption Certificate as evidence of her income.

26   In order to claim, a woman may need to provide a .... as
     evidence of the due date.

27   Payment may be affected by differences in someone's .... ,
     such as a return to work, and the local Jobcentre Plus must be informed.

→ ◳ p. 122   23

SECTION 3   *Questions 28–40*

Read the text below and answer Questions 28–40.

The California Gold Rush of 1849

The discovery of gold in the Sacramento Valley sparked the Gold Rush, arguably one of the most significant events to shape American history in the 19th century

A   On January 24, 1848, James Wilson Marshall, a carpenter, found small flakes of gold in the American River near Coloma, California. At the time, Marshall was working to build a water-powered sawmill for businessman John Sutter. As it happens, just days after Marshall's discovery, the Treaty of Guadalupe Hidalgo was signed, ending the Mexican–American War and transferring California, with its mineral deposits, into the ownership of the United States. At the time, the population of the territory consisted of 6,500 Californios (people of Spanish or Mexican descent); 700 foreigners (primarily Americans); and 150,000 Native Americans.

B   Though Marshall and Sutter tried to keep news of the discovery quiet, word got out, and by mid-March 1848 at least one newspaper was reporting that large quantities of gold were being found. Though the initial reaction in San Francisco was disbelief, storekeeper Sam Brannan set off a frenzy when he paraded through town displaying a small bottle containing gold from Sutter's Creek. By mid-June, some three-quarters of the male population of San Francisco had left town for the gold mines, and the number of miners in the area reached 4,000 by August.

C   As news spread of the fortunes being made in California, the first migrants to arrive were those from lands accessible by boat, such as Oregon, the Sandwich Islands (now Hawaii), Mexico, Chile, Peru and even China. Only later would the news reach the East Coast, where press reports were initially skeptical. Throughout 1849, thousands of people around the United States (mostly men) borrowed money, mortgaged their property or spent their life savings to make the arduous journey to California. In pursuit of the kind of wealth they had never dreamed of, they left their families and local areas; in turn, their wives had no option but to shoulder different responsibilities such as running farms or businesses, and many made a real success of them.

By the end of the year, the non-native population of California was estimated at 100,000 (as compared with 20,000 at the end of 1848 and around 800 in March 1848). To accommodate the needs of the '49ers, as the gold miners were known, towns had sprung up all over the region, complete with shops and other businesses seeking to make their own Gold Rush fortune. The overcrowded chaos of the mining camps and towns grew ever more lawless. San Francisco, for its part, developed a bustling economy and became the central metropolis of the new frontier.

D How did all these would-be miners search for gold? Panning was the oldest way. The basic procedure was to place some gold-bearing materials, such as river gravel, into a shallow pan, add some water, and then carefully swirl the mixture around so the water and light material spilled over the side. If all went well, the heavier gold nuggets or gold dust would settle to the bottom of the pan. Gold panning was slow even for the most skillful miner. On a good day, one miner could wash about 50 pans in the usual 12-hour workday.

E Another way was to use what was called a 'rocker'. Isaac Humphrey is said to have introduced it to the California gold fields. It was simply a rectangular wooden box, set at a downward angle and mounted on a rocking mechanism. The dirt and rock was dumped into the top, followed by a bucket of water. The box was rocked by hand to agitate the mixture. The big rocks were caught in a sieve at the top, the waste exited the lower end with the water, and the heavy gold fell to the bottom of the box.

The rocker had advantages and disadvantages. The advantages were that it was easily transportable; it did not require a constant source of water; and, most importantly, a miner could process more dirt and rock than with a pan. The primary disadvantage was that the rocker had difficulty in trapping the smallest particles of gold, commonly known as 'flour'. Some miners added small amounts of mercury to the bottom of the rocker. Due to its chemical composition, it had a facility to trap fine gold. Periodically, the miners would remove and heat it. As it vaporized, it would leave gold behind.

F After 1850, the surface gold in California had largely disappeared, even as miners continued to reach the gold fields. Mining had always been difficult and dangerous labor, and striking it rich required good luck as much as skill and hard work. Moreover, the average daily pay for an independent miner had by then dropped sharply from what it had been in 1848. As gold became more and more difficult to reach, the growing industrialization of mining drove more and more miners from independence into wage labor. The new technique of hydraulic mining, developed in 1853, brought enormous profits, but destroyed much of the region's landscape.

G Though gold mining continued throughout the 1850s, it had reached its peak by 1852, when gold worth some $81 million was pulled from the ground. After that year, the total take declined gradually, leveling off to around $45 million per year by 1857. Settlement in California continued, however, and by the end of the decade the state's population was 380,000.

Questions 28–31

*Choose the correct letter, **A**, **B**, **C** or **D**.*

Write the correct letter in boxes 28–31 on your answer sheet.

28 The writer suggests that Marshall's discovery came at a good time for the US because

    A   the Mexican–American War was ending so there were men needing work.
    B   his expertise in water power would be useful in gold mining.
    C   the population of California had already begun to increase rapidly.
    D   the region was about to come under the control of the US.

29 What was the reaction in 1848 to the news of the discovery of gold?

    A   The press played a large part in convincing the public of the riches available.
    B   Many men in San Francisco left immediately to check it out for themselves.
    C   People needed to see physical evidence before they took it seriously.
    D   Men in other mines in the US were among the first to respond to it.

30 What was the result of thousands of people moving to California?

    A   San Francisco could not cope with the influx of people from around the world.
    B   Many miners got more money than they could ever have earned at home.
    C   Some of those who stayed behind had to take on unexpected roles.
    D   New towns were established which became good places to live.

31 What does the writer say about using pans and rockers to find gold?

    A   Both methods required the addition of mercury.
    B   A rocker needed more than one miner to operate it.
    C   Pans were the best system for novice miners to use.
    D   Miners had to find a way round a design fault in one system.

Questions 32–36

The text on pages 24 and 25 has seven sections, **A–G**.

Which section contains the following information?

*Write the correct letter, **A–G**, in boxes 32–36 on your answer sheet.*

32 a reference to ways of making money in California other than mining for gold

33 a suggestion that the gold that was found did not often compensate for the hard work undertaken

34 a mention of an individual who convinced many of the existence of gold in California

35 details of the pre-Gold Rush population of California

36 a contrast between shrinking revenue and increasing population

Questions 37–40

Complete the summary below.

*Choose **ONE WORD ONLY** from the text for each answer.*

Write your answers in boxes 37–40 on your answer sheet.

Basic techniques for extracting gold

The most basic method used by many miners began with digging some
37 .... out of a river and hoping it might contain gold. Small amounts were
put in a pan with water. The pan was spun round, causing the liquid and less heavy
contents of the pan to come out. Gold dust, which weighed more, remained in the pan
or, if the miners were very lucky, there might even be some **38** .... too.
It was, however, a very laborious method.

The rocker was also used. A miner would put some earth and rock into the higher end,
together with some water. He would then shake the rocker. Larger stones stuck in the
39 .... , while gold dropped to the bottom. Unfortunately, the rocker
was not designed to catch what was called flour. However, a process was introduced
involving **40** .... to ensure no gold was washed out in the water.

WRITING

WRITING TASK 1

You should spend about 20 minutes on this task.

> *A friend of yours is thinking of going on a camping holiday for the first time this summer. He/She has asked for your advice.*
>
> *Write a letter to your friend. In your letter*
> - *explain why you think your friend would enjoy a camping holiday*
> - *describe some possible disadvantages*
> - *say whether you would like to go camping with your friend this summer*

Write at least 150 words.

You do **NOT** need to write any addresses.

Begin your letter as follows:

Dear .... ,

→ ✎ p. 129

WRITING TASK 2

You should spend about 40 minutes on this task.

Write about the following topic:

In many countries today, crime novels and TV crime dramas are becoming more and more popular.

Why do you think these books and TV shows are popular?

What is your opinion of crime fiction and TV crime dramas?

Give reasons for your answer and include any relevant examples from your own knowledge or experience.

Write at least 250 words.

 → p. 130

SPEAKING

PART 1

The examiner asks the candidate about him/herself, his/her home, work or studies and other familiar topics.

Example Speaking test video

EXAMPLE

Email

- What kinds of emails do you receive about your work or studies?
- Do you prefer to email, phone or text your friends? [Why?]
- Do you reply to emails and messages as soon as you receive them? [Why/Why not?]
- Are you happy to receive emails that are advertising things? [Why/Why not?]

PART 2

Describe a hotel that you know.
 	
You should say:
    where this hotel is
    what this hotel looks like
    what facilities this hotel has
 	
and explain whether you think this is a nice hotel to stay in.

You will have to talk about the topic for one to two minutes. You have one minute to think about what you are going to say. You can make some notes to help you if you wish.

PART 3

Discussion topics:

Staying in hotels

Example questions:
What things are important when people are choosing a hotel?
Why do some people not like staying in hotels?
Do you think staying in a luxury hotel is a waste of money?

Working in a hotel

Example questions:
Do you think hotel work is a good career for life?
How does working in a big hotel compare with working in a small hotel?
What skills are needed to be a successful hotel manager?

Test 2

PART 1   Questions 1–10

Questions 1–4

Complete the table below.

Write **ONE WORD ONLY** for each answer.

Listening test audio

Festival information		
Date	**Type of event**	**Details**
17th	a concert	performers from Canada
18th	a ballet	company called **1** ....
19th–20th (afternoon)	a play	type of play: a comedy called *Jemima* has had a good **2** ....
20th (evening)	a **3** .... show	show is called **4** ....

Questions 5–10

Complete the notes below.

Write **ONE WORD ONLY** for each answer.

Workshops

- Making **5** .... food

- (children only) Making **6** ....

- (adults only) Making toys from **7** .... using various tools

Outdoor activities

- Swimming in the **8** ....

- Walking in the woods, led by an expert on **9** ....

See the festival organiser's **10** .... for more information

PART 2 *Questions 11–20*

Questions 11–14

Choose the correct letter, A, B or C.

Listening test audio

Minster Park

11   The park was originally established

    A   as an amenity provided by the city council.
    B   as land belonging to a private house.
    C   as a shared area set up by the local community.

12   Why is there a statue of Diane Gosforth in the park?

    A   She was a resident who helped to lead a campaign.
    B   She was a council member responsible for giving the public access.
    C   She was a senior worker at the park for many years.

13   During the First World War, the park was mainly used for

    A   exercises by troops.
    B   growing vegetables.
    C   public meetings.

14   When did the physical transformation of the park begin?

    A   2013
    B   2015
    C   2016

Questions 15–20

Label the map below.

*Write the correct letter, **A–I**, next to Questions 15–20.*

Minster Park

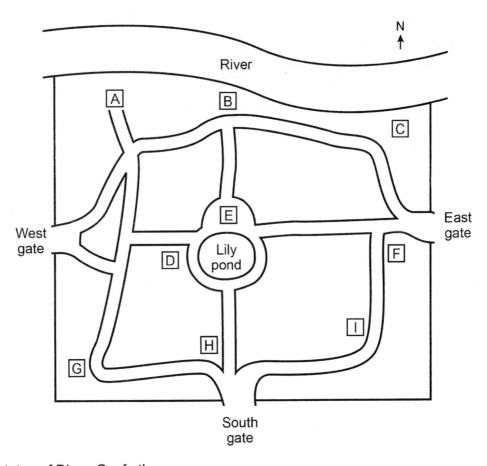

15 statue of Diane Gosforth   ....

16 wooden sculptures   ....

17 playground   ....

18 maze   ....

19 tennis courts   ....

20 fitness area   ....

PART 3   *Questions 21–30*

Questions 21 and 22

Listening test audio

*Choose **TWO** letters, **A–E**.*

Which **TWO** groups of people is the display primarily intended for?

A	students from the English department
B	residents of the local area
C	the university's teaching staff
D	potential new students
E	students from other departments

Questions 23 and 24

*Choose **TWO** letters, **A–E**.*

What are Cathy and Graham's **TWO** reasons for choosing the novelist Charles Dickens?

A	His speeches inspired others to try to improve society.
B	He used his publications to draw attention to social problems.
C	His novels are well-known now.
D	He was consulted on a number of social issues.
E	His reputation has changed in recent times.

Questions 25–30

What topic do Cathy and Graham choose to illustrate with each novel?

*Choose **SIX** answers from the box and write the correct letter, **A–H**, next to Questions 25–30.*

Topics	
A	poverty
B	education
C	Dickens's travels
D	entertainment
E	crime and the law
F	wealth
G	medicine
H	a woman's life

Novels by Dickens

25	*The Pickwick Papers*	....
26	*Oliver Twist*	....
27	*Nicholas Nickleby*	....
28	*Martin Chuzzlewit*	....
29	*Bleak House*	....
30	*Little Dorrit*	....

 → ◓ p. 123 ▤ p. 105

PART 4   *Questions 31–40*

Complete the notes below.

*Write **ONE WORD ONLY** for each answer.*

Listening test audio

Agricultural programme in Mozambique

How the programme was organised

- It focused on a dry and arid region in Chicualacuala district, near the Limpopo River.

- People depended on the forest to provide charcoal as a source of income.

- **31** .... was seen as the main priority to ensure the supply of water.

- Most of the work organised by farmers' associations was done by
  32 ....

- Fenced areas were created to keep animals away from crops.

- The programme provided

  – **33** .... for the fences

  – **34** .... for suitable crops

  – water pumps.

- The farmers provided

  – labour

  – **35** .... for the fences on their land.

Further developments

- The marketing of produce was sometimes difficult due to lack of
  36 ....

- Training was therefore provided in methods of food **37** ....

- Farmers made special places where **38** .... could be kept.

- Local people later suggested keeping **39** ....

Evaluation and lessons learned

- Agricultural production increased, improving incomes and food security.

- Enough time must be allowed, particularly for the **40** .... phase of
  the programme.

SECTION 1   *Questions 1–14*

Read the text below and answer Questions 1–6.

Harvey's Storage

Harvey's Storage is a well-established independent company. We are centrally located in the city and provide excellent facilities for all your storage requirements.

We provide safe and secure units for both long- and short-term storage dependent on your needs. Our rates are competitive and tailored to your specific requirements and your choice of storage unit. Heavy-duty locks and keys are provided to all of our customers and included in the prices listed. You can hire the unit with the storage capacity you need, for the period of time that the storage is required, in a sound and secure environment, monitored by CCTV. With 24-hour access, customers can deliver and collect items when it is convenient to do so, unrestricted by business or office hours. Tarmac roadways allow customers to park cars and lorries immediately outside their units, minimising the effort required to collect or drop items off.

Household storage Self-storage is ideal for families or individuals with either a short- or long-term need to store their belongings. Some of our clients are de-cluttering, or they may be getting their property decorated, or planning to go abroad for a time.

Student storage You may be travelling or going home to see family and friends in the vacation, or need time to find a place to stay. You may want to store all your books and personal items, or just a few boxes or a musical instrument. We offer no-nonsense competitive pricing with flexible hire periods and with no hidden extras. We can provide you with short- or long-term affordable hire in a safe and secure environment. You are responsible for organising transport but we can also recommend local van and driver hire companies.

Business storage Free up your expensive retail space with affordable self-storage. We have three different business storage centres to choose from so you can choose the location that is most convenient for you.

Questions 1–6

Do the following statements agree with the information given in the text on page 38?

In boxes 1–6 on your answer sheet, write

> **TRUE**   *if the statement agrees with the information*
> **FALSE**   *if the statement contradicts the information*
> **NOT GIVEN**   *if there is no information on this*

1   There is an extra charge for locks and keys.

2   It is possible to arrange to share a storage unit with someone else.

3   You can pick up your property from the storage unit during the night-time.

4   You can drive your vehicle right next to your storage unit.

5   Students' possessions can only be stored during vacation periods.

6   The storage company will collect and deliver students' property.

Read the text below and answer Questions 7–14.

Local museums

A **Whittlesey Museum**

The museum is located in the Old Town Hall, which was originally built to house horse-drawn fire engines. It has eight rooms, and the exhibits cover topics such as archive photographs, costume, domestic life and local celebrities.

B **Octavia Hill's Birthplace House**

Built in 1740, this is the birthplace of pioneer social reformer Octavia Hill, who was active in the late 19th and early 20th centuries in social housing and the arts, as well as in conservation issues. Visitors are taken on a guided tour and are then free to explore the gardens.

C **Chatteris Museum**

The old market town of Chatteris was largely rebuilt, after two serious fires in 1706 and 1864 destroyed many of the town's ancient buildings. The museum's exhibits illustrate traditional aspects of the life of local farmers as well as the railway boom of the 19th century. The museum has a touch-screen kiosk which contains over 9,000 historic photographs and texts, reproductions of which can be made on request.

D **March and District Museum**

Located in the middle of the market town of March, the museum is housed in a former school built in 1851. Its wide-ranging collections include reconstructions of an early 20th-century kitchen, sitting room and nursery. There is also an interesting display of historic cameras and radios, and a medal which was awarded to train driver Ben Gimbert for his bravery in preventing loss of life when a train full of explosives caught fire in 1944.

E **Wisbech and Fenland Museum**

This 19th-century gem holds collections from around the world including Ancient Egypt. Its library, which is open to the public on the first Saturday of each month, contains the manuscript of *Great Expectations* by the 19th-century novelist Charles Dickens, and the Research Room can be booked for researching local records.

Questions 7–14

*Look at the five descriptions of museums, **A–E**, in one area of England, on page 40.*

For which museum are the following statements true?

*Write the correct letter, **A–E**, in boxes 7–14 on your answer sheet.*

NB *You may use any letter more than once.*

7   There are exhibits related to the history of agriculture in the region.

8   Equipment for putting out fires used to be kept in this building.

9   You can find information on the rise of one type of transport.

10   There are things to see both inside and outside.

11   It is possible to obtain copies of old pictures and documents.

12   On certain days you can see an original work by a writer of fiction.

13   Someone who was interested in environmental matters lived here for a time.

14   This museum has an exhibit related to a heroic achievement.

→ ◍ p. 124

SECTION 2   *Questions 15–27*

Read the text below and answer Questions 15–20.

Workplace health and safety considerations for plumbers

Like many trades, plumbing can be a dangerous job. It is important to take all reasonably practicable measures to keep customers and yourself incident and injury free.

Biohazard waste

Plumbers regularly come into contact with biohazard waste. It's the nature of the job, but that doesn't mean you should be complacent about it. According to Safe Work Australia, communicable diseases from work-related exposures to biological hazards such as sewage have been estimated to cause 320,000 deaths across the globe each year. In addition to this, plumbers are regularly exposed to other biohazards such as mould, bacteria and algae. Don't risk it – make sure appropriate protective clothing and equipment is used.

Confined spaces

Plumbers may spend much of their time working in confined spaces, where they are at risk from contaminants, including airborne gases, vapours and dusts, that may cause injury from fire or explosion. They may also be exposed to high concentrations of airborne contaminants that may be harmful to health. For example, one plumber was fined $220,000 after an employee suffered from carbon-monoxide poisoning. Another potential hazard for plumbers in confined spaces is that of drowning, if water sources are not adequately cut off.

The Safe Work Australia confined spaces code of practice outlines the necessary steps and precautions for avoiding illness and injury.

Electricity

The Master Plumbers' Association calls electricity 'plumbing's hidden killer'. Metal pipes are often conductive and so gloves which provide insulation should form part of a plumber's tool kit, as should a plumbing voltage monitor and a volt tester. Gloves should be checked prior to every use and replaced every 12 to 14 months. Electrical equipment like bridging conductors should be regularly checked, with appropriate tags on the equipment to verify its safety. The project should be stopped immediately if there is any sign of electricity, so that the power can be disconnected by a qualified electrician prior to continuing work.

Questions 15–20

Complete the table below.

*Choose **ONE WORD ONLY** from the text for each answer.*

Write your answers in boxes 15–20 on your answer sheet.

Type of danger	Examples	Risks involved	Necessary action
Biohazard	15 ...., mould, bacteria, algae	can lead to disease and death	use protective clothing and equipment
Confined spaces	contaminants e.g. gases, vapours and dusts	injury from fire or explosion	follow Safe Work code of practice
	high concentrations of harmful airborne contaminants e.g. carbon monoxide	16	follow Safe Work code of practice
	water	17	cut off water sources
Electricity	metal pipes which are conductive	death from electrocution	– use insulated 18 .... and appropriate equipment – ensure equipment has 19 .... on to show it is safe – make sure electricity has been 20 ....

Read the text below and answer Questions 21–27.

How to manage flexible working with your employees

There is no denying that flexible working has grown enormously in recent years. It does, however, require careful management.

When it comes to implementing flexible working one word is key: trust. All flexible workers should be trusted and given well-defined objectives from the start and their contribution should be assessed according to their output, as opposed to the time they spend on the job. It can be a big step to implement such a change in your business, so if you are slightly cautious then I recommend perhaps setting up an end-of-the-day review to see how much progress has been made. As all parties find their feet with the new set-up, this contact can slowly be reduced.

In my eyes, it is also vital that there is shared calendar access for everyone so that people can see where their colleagues are each day. This way if they need to catch up with someone they can plan when to do so. Technology now exists to enable employees to stay in touch with other members of staff and external partners. iMeet, for example, is a tool which allows all forms of collaboration for remote working, from video conferencing, live chat and file sharing to screen sharing. The new breed of worker is therefore fully equipped to work productively away from the office, and can still feel like they're in the same room as others when necessary.

In my experience, employees are often more productive working at home as they can work the exact hours they want and do not have to cope with distraction caused by other employees. Being outside the confines of the office walls also appears to foster creativity. In addition, we find staff are more motivated as they have a better work–life balance. In terms of the business, we find this helps with top talent recruitment and staff retention, and a happy workforce is a more successful one.

Questions 21–27

Complete the notes below.

*Choose **ONE WORD ONLY** from the text for each answer.*

Write your answers in boxes 21–27 on your answer sheet.

Flexible working

How to organise flexible working

- trust your employees

- provide them with clear **21** ....

- base measurements of performance on their output

- initially, have a **22** .... of progress each day

- make sure a **23** .... is accessible to give details of colleague locations

- use a program such as iMeet to encourage different types of **24** .... between workers

Benefits of flexibility

- greater productivity

- less **25** .... from colleagues

- increase in **26** ....

- more motivated staff

- greater success for the company with staff recruitment and **27** ....

→ 🔊 p. 124

SECTION 3 *Questions 28–40*

Read the text on pages 47 and 48 and answer Questions 28–40.

Questions 28–33

The text on pages 47 and 48 has six sections, **A–F**.

Choose the correct heading for each section from the list of headings below.

*Write the correct number, **i–vii**, in boxes 28–33 on your answer sheet.*

List of Headings

  i   Developing an item that appears true to life

  ii   Extending the project to other endangered species

  iii A short but intensive investigation with longer-term follow-up

  iv Problems facing sea turtles at a global level

  v   Collection of eggs and their possible onward routes

  vi Intensive and large-scale poaching in one location

  vii Why catching the poachers may not solve the problem

---

28   Section **A**

29   Section **B**

30   Section **C**

31   Section **D**

32   Section **E**

33   Section **F**

Preventing the theft of turtle eggs

Conservationists and law enforcement have struggled to prevent wildlife trafficking. But could some plastic eggs and GPS trackers change the game?

A   Humans have been eating sea turtle eggs (and killing adult turtles for meat) for millennia. However, as human populations exploded and as sea turtles began to confront additional threats such as intensive fishing, beach development and climate change, sea turtle populations declined precipitously. Today, all but one of the world's seven species of sea turtles are considered threatened according to the IUCN* Red List. And the one that's not – the flatback turtle – is listed as data deficient, which means scientists simply don't know how it's doing.

B   One major problem is that every year millions of sea turtle eggs are illegally taken by poachers for sale on the black market. The situation is particularly serious in Nicaragua, in Central America, which is home to four sea turtle species.

Kim Williams-Guillen, who works for conservation body Paso Pacifico, described the poaching of sea turtle nests on the beaches of Nicaragua as 'uncontrolled, unregulated, extensive and contested'. Even the best-protected beaches are plundered to some extent and it's not uncommon to see poachers digging up nests just meters from tourists watching sea turtles laying their clutch at night, she said. This poaching becomes particularly frenzied during the *arribadas* – mass laying events where thousands of turtles nest on the same beach for a single night in a biological strategy to overwhelm natural predators.

C   'Even with armed guards, the numbers of poachers overwhelm military personnel by ten or twenty to one,' Williams-Guillen said. 'Although many poachers are locals with limited resources, during these *arribadas* there are influxes of gangs of poachers from larger cities outside local communities. These are not just local poor people without other options.'

But to protect the country's sea turtles, Williams-Guillen said conservationists shouldn't just depend on catching low-level operators. 'If one poacher decides to stop, another one will just step into his place … we need to know more about the middlemen and people higher up in the distribution chain,' she said.

D   Paso Pacifico's solution is the creation of high-tech sea turtle eggs: fake eggs convincingly crafted to look like the real thing, but which contain GPS tracking devices. These have the potential to reveal the destination markets for trafficked sea turtle eggs.

---

*IUCN: International Union for Conservation of Nature

Making convincing sea turtle eggs is not easy, and Paso Pacifico is still working on perfecting a prototype. In particular, it's proving quite problematic to create the right texture, since sea turtle eggs are not covered in a hard shell like those of birds, but are quite flexible.

So Paso Pacifico brought in Lauren Wilde, a special effects artist in the US, to create a convincing outer shell. First, Wilde had to get her hands on the real thing. Since it's illegal to send sea turtle eggs over the border, Wilde is using land turtle eggs from California. 'It was really eye opening and important for me to feel these eggs and how the shell bends a little,' she said.

To get the GPS device inside the shell, Paso Pacifico is using 3D printers to make a plastic ball which will then have a GPS transmitter fitted inside. This will take the place of the embryo inside the shell. Lastly the fake shells will be sealed with silicone, waterproofing them.

E   Sea turtles on average lay around 100 eggs in a nest, and once the fake eggs are finished they will be slipped in with the real ones. Williams-Guillen said it might even be possible to deliver fake eggs into nests while poachers are at work. Wary of tourists, poachers will often back off if strangers come near and then return when they have gone. 'It would be pretty easy to drop an egg in the dark into a nest they have been digging up,' she said.

Once the poacher picks up the fake egg along with the real ones, conservationists and law enforcement agents will be able to track them. Experts believe most of the stolen eggs eventually make their way out of Nicaragua, possibly to El Salvador or Guatemala. However, there is also growing concern that sea turtle eggs from Central America are actually heading to the USA, from where they are sold on to other countries around the world.

F   To date, Paso Pacifico has yet to put a single fake egg in a nest. But Williams-Guillen said she isn't too concerned that publicity for their scheme will result in poachers looking for the eggs. 'The vast majority of the poaching is happening at night, so already it is hard to tell [the eggs] apart, and at this point, poachers and middlemen are not closely inspecting eggs, but rather shoving them into a sack as quickly as possible.'

Of course, poachers will eventually become aware of the prospect of fake eggs among the real ones – especially when customers try to bite into an egg and break their teeth on the GPS transmitter instead. So, Paso Pacifico plans to do a massive deployment of as many fakes as possible to gather a lot of data before poachers get wise.

Knowing where the eggs go will allow conservationists and law enforcement agents to focus their resources on the right places – whether it be through awareness-building campaigns or crackdowns on illegal sellers. And eventually Paso Pacifico hopes to share the technology with interested parties around the world.

Questions 34–37

*Choose the correct letter, **A, B, C** or **D**.*

Write the correct letter in boxes 34–37 on your answer sheet.

34   What does the writer suggest about the flatback turtle?

    A   It could be as severely threatened as other turtles.
    B   It has been neglected by scientists in the past.
    C   It is in less danger than some other species.
    D   It should be removed from the IUCN Red List.

35   Williams-Guillen says that the poaching of sea turtle eggs in Nicaragua

    A   is mainly carried out by local people.
    B   may be encouraged by the presence of tourists.
    C   sometimes has a highly organised structure.
    D   can only be controlled by the use of armed guards.

36   In Section E, Williams-Guillen says that one way to encourage poachers to take the fake eggs is to

    A   make fake nests and put the eggs into them.
    B   put them in nests with just a few real eggs.
    C   distract the poachers after the fake eggs have been put in the nests.
    D   put them in nests that the poachers have started to dig up.

37   It is planned to use a large number of fake eggs at the beginning because

    A   some of the fake eggs may be missed by the poachers.
    B   it may not be possible to continue the project indefinitely.
    C   some eggs may be hidden in the sand.
    D   it may not be feasible to fund long-term research.

Questions 38–40

Complete the summary below.

*Choose **ONE WORD ONLY** from the text for each answer.*

Write your answers in boxes 38–40 on your answer sheet.

Making convincing sea turtle eggs

One difficulty in creating a fake sea turtle egg is to get the appropriate texture for the shell. Unlike a bird's egg, a turtle's egg has a shell which is **38** .... Lauren Wilde has studied eggs from Californian turtles that live on **39** .... to create a realistic reproduction of the shell. A GPS device will then be placed inside a **40** .... in the fake shell. Finally, silicone will be applied to the shell to make it waterproof.

WRITING TASK 1

You should spend about 20 minutes on this task.

A museum near your home is looking for people to do part-time voluntary/unpaid work. You would like to do some voluntary/unpaid work at the museum.

Write a letter to the museum director to apply for the voluntary/unpaid work. In your letter

- *explain why you want to do voluntary/unpaid work at the museum*
- *describe some skills and qualities you have that would be useful*
- *give details of when you would be available for work*

Write at least 150 words.

You do **NOT** need to write any addresses.

Begin your letter as follows:

Dear Sir or Madam,

WRITING TASK 2

You should spend about 40 minutes on this task.

Write about the following topic:

> **Nowadays many people complain that they have difficulties getting enough sleep.**
>
> **What problems can lack of sleep cause?**
>
> **What can be done about lack of sleep?**

Give reasons for your answer and include any relevant examples from your own knowledge or experience.

Write at least 250 words.

PART 1

The examiner asks the candidate about him/herself, his/her home, work or studies and other familiar topics.

EXAMPLE

Languages

- How many languages can you speak? [Why/Why not?]
- How useful will English be to you in your future? [Why/Why not?]
- What do you remember about learning languages at school? [Why/Why not?]
- What do you think would be the hardest language for you to learn? [Why?]

PART 2

Describe a website that you bought something from.
 	
You should say:
    what the website is
    what you bought from this website
    how satisfied you were with what you bought
 	
and explain what you liked or disliked about using this website.

You will have to talk about the topic for one to two minutes. You have one minute to think about what you are going to say. You can make some notes to help you if you wish.

PART 3

Discussion topics:

Shopping online

Example questions:
What kinds of things do people in your country often buy from online shops?
Why do you think online shopping has become so popular nowadays?
What are some possible disadvantages of buying things from online shops?

The culture of consumerism

Example questions:
Why do many people today keep buying things which they do not need?
Do you believe the benefits of a consumer society outweigh the disadvantages?
How possible is it to avoid the culture of consumerism?

Test 3

PART 1   *Questions 1–10*

Complete the notes below.

*Write **ONE WORD AND/OR A NUMBER** for each answer.*

Listening test audio

Employment Agency: Possible Jobs

First Job

Administrative assistant in a company that produces **1** .... (North London)

Responsibilities

- data entry
- go to **2** .... and take notes
- general admin
- management of **3** ....

Requirements

- good computer skills including spreadsheets
- good interpersonal skills
- attention to **4** ....

Experience

- need a minimum of **5** .... of experience of teleconferencing

---

Second Job

Warehouse assistant in South London

Responsibilities

- stock management
- managing **6** ....

Requirements

- ability to work with numbers
- good computer skills
- very organised and **7** ....
- good communication skills
- used to working in a **8** ....
- able to cope with items that are **9** ....

Need experience of

- driving in London
- warehouse work
- **10** .... service

PART 2   *Questions 11–20*

Questions 11–16

Choose the correct letter, A, B or C.

Listening test audio

Street Play Scheme

11 When did the Street Play Scheme first take place?

   A   two years ago
   B   three years ago
   C   six years ago

12 How often is Beechwood Road closed to traffic now?

   A   once a week
   B   on Saturdays and Sundays
   C   once a month

13 Who is responsible for closing the road?

   A   a council official
   B   the police
   C   local wardens

14 Residents who want to use their cars

   A   have to park in another street.
   B   must drive very slowly.
   C   need permission from a warden.

15 Alice says that Street Play Schemes are most needed in

   A   wealthy areas.
   B   quiet suburban areas.
   C   areas with heavy traffic.

16 What has been the reaction of residents who are not parents?

   A   Many of them were unhappy at first.
   B   They like seeing children play in the street.
   C   They are surprised by the lack of noise.

Questions 17 and 18

*Choose **TWO** letters, **A–E**.*

Which **TWO** benefits for children does Alice think are the most important?

    A   increased physical activity
    B   increased sense of independence
    C   opportunity to learn new games
    D   opportunity to be part of a community
    E   opportunity to make new friends

Questions 19 and 20

*Choose **TWO** letters, **A–E**.*

Which **TWO** results of the King Street experiment surprised Alice?

    A   more shoppers
    B   improved safety
    C   less air pollution
    D   more relaxed atmosphere
    E   less noise pollution

PART 3   *Questions 21–30*

Questions 21–26

Complete the notes below.

*Write **ONE WORD ONLY** for each answer.*

Listening test audio

What Hazel should analyse about items in newspapers:

- what **21** .... the item is on

- the **22** .... of the item, including the headline

- any **23** .... accompanying the item

- the **24** .... of the item, e.g. what's made prominent

- the writer's main **25** ....

- the **26** .... the writer may make about the reader

Questions 27–30

What does Hazel decide to do about each of the following types of articles?

*Write the correct letter, **A, B** or **C**, next to Questions 27–30.*

A	She will definitely look for a suitable article.
B	She may look for a suitable article.
C	She definitely won't look for an article.

Types of articles

27 national news item   ....

28 editorial   ....

29 human interest   ....

30 arts   ....

PART 4   *Questions 31–40*

Listening test audio

Complete the notes below.

*Write **ONE WORD ONLY** for each answer.*

Early history of keeping clean

Prehistoric times:

- water was used to wash off **31** ....

Ancient Babylon:

- soap-like material found in **32** .... cylinders

Ancient Greece:

- people cleaned themselves with sand and other substances

- used a strigil – scraper made of **33** ....

- washed clothes in streams

Ancient Germany and Gaul:

- used soap to colour their **34** ....

Ancient Rome:

- animal fat, ashes and clay mixed through action of rain, used for washing clothes

- from about 312 BC, water carried to Roman **35** .... by aqueducts

Europe in Middle Ages:

- decline in bathing contributed to occurrence of **36** ....

- **37** .... began to be added to soap

Europe from 17th century:

- 1600s: cleanliness and bathing started becoming usual

- 1791: Leblanc invented a way of making soda ash from **38** ....

- early 1800s: Chevreul turned soapmaking into a **39** ....

- from 1800s, there was no longer a **40** .... on soap

→ 🔊 p. 125 | 📄 p. 113

READING

SECTION 1   *Questions 1–14*

Read the text below and answer Questions 1–7.

Young Fashion Designer UK competition

Young Fashion Designer UK is an exciting national competition which aims to showcase and promote the exceptional work achieved by students studying courses in textile design, product design and fashion throughout the UK.

The competition is designed for students to enter the coursework they are currently working on rather than specifically producing different pieces of work. If you would like to add to your coursework, that is for you and your teacher to decide.

You can apply independently or through your school/college. To enter please ensure you follow these steps:

1) Provide three A3 colour copies from your design folder.

    You must include:

    – initial ideas about the clothing

    – a close-up photograph of the front and back view of the finished clothing.

2) Please label each sheet clearly with your name and school (on the back).

3) Print off a copy of your registration form and attach it to your work.

4) Post your entry to the Young Fashion Designer Centre.

Once the entry deadline has passed, the judges will select the shortlist of students who will be invited to the Finals. You will be notified if you are shortlisted. You will need to bring originals of the work that you entered. Each finalist will have their own stand consisting of a table and tabletop cardboard display panels. Feel free to add as much creativity to your stand as possible. Some students bring tablets/laptops with slideshows or further images of work but it should be emphasised that these may not necessarily improve your chances of success.

The judges will assess your work and will ask various questions about it. They will look through any supporting information and the work you have on display before coming together as a judging panel to decide on the winners. You are welcome to ask the judges questions. In fact, you should make the most of having experts on hand!

There are 1st, 2nd and 3rd prize winners for each category. The judges can also decide to award special prizes if the work merits this. The 1st, 2nd and 3rd place winners will receive a glass trophy and prize from a kind donor.

Questions 1–7

Do the following statements agree with the information given in the text on page 60?

In boxes 1–7 on your answer sheet, write

> **TRUE**   *if the statement agrees with the information*
> **FALSE**   *if the statement contradicts the information*
> **NOT GIVEN** *if there is no information on this*

1   Participants are required to create a new item of clothing for the Young Fashion Designer UK competition.

2   Participants must send information about the thoughts that led to the item they are entering for the competition.

3   The shortlist will consist of a fixed number of finalists.

4   Finalists can choose how to present their work to the judges on their stand.

5   It is strongly recommended that finalists support their entry with additional photographs.

6   Questions that the students ask the judges may count towards the final decisions.

7   Extra prizes may be awarded depending on the standard of the entries submitted.

Read the text below and answer Questions 8–14.

Which keyboard should you buy?

It's worth remembering that a bad keyboard can significantly affect your entire computing experience. So make sure you pick the right keyboard for your needs.

A   Logitech K120

Logitech's K120 offers a number of extra features. It's spill-resistant, draining small amounts of liquid if you have an accident. It isn't particularly eye-catching, but it feels very solid. For the price, it's a tempting choice.

B   Cherry MX 3.0 Keyboard

The Cherry MX 3.0 looks simple and neat, thanks to its compact build. It's solid, durable and you don't need to push keys all the way down to activate them. It's also rather loud though, which can take some getting used to.

C   Logitech K780

The K780 is a compact, pleasantly modern-looking keyboard. There's an integrated stand for smartphones and tablets too. It's quiet to type on, and the circular keys are easy to familiarise yourself with, well-spaced and large enough to hit accurately. For this price though, the lack of backlighting is disappointing.

D   Microsoft Sculpt Ergonomic

The Sculpt's curved, strange-looking build serves a purpose. It provides wrist support and lifts your forearms into a relaxed position so you don't hurt yourself from typing for lengthy periods. It feels weird, but it seems to do the trick.

E   Microsoft Universal Bluetooth Keyboard

Microsoft's Bluetooth keyboard has one very handy feature – you can fold it in half and carry it around in your jacket pocket or bag, and it feels rather like a large wallet. It has generously sized keys, though the two-piece spacebar takes some getting used to. Another useful feature is that you can get up to three months' use from a single charge.

F   Corsair Strafe RGB Keyboard

Corsair's keyboard is expensive, flashy and extremely impressive. All of its keys are programmable, there's eye-catching backlighting and the buttons are textured for improved grip. All this is because it's designed for gamers. However, it's also silent, meaning it is suitable for everyday office work too.

Questions 8–14

*Look at the six reviews of computer keyboards, **A–F**, on page 62.*

For which keyboard are the following statements true?

*Write the correct letter, **A–F**, in boxes 8–14 on your answer sheet.*

NB *You may use any letter more than once.*

8   This keyboard may not suit users who prefer the keys to be almost silent.

9   This keyboard is easily portable because it can be made to fit into a small space.

10   This keyboard includes a special place to put small devices.

11   This keyboard is designed to prevent injury to those who spend a lot of time on the computer.

12   This keyboard offers good value for money.

13   This keyboard is primarily aimed at people who use their computer for entertainment.

14   It shouldn't take long for users to get used to the shape of the keys on this keyboard.

→ p. 126

SECTION 2   *Questions 15–27*

Read the text below and answer Questions 15–20.

Working for a small company may be better than you think

Recent research shows that many job-seekers believe their ideal position would be in a large company. However, working for a small or medium-sized business has many advantages that are too easily overlooked. Here are just a few of them.

Working in a small organisation with a small workforce means it's likely to be easy to become part of it. It won't be long before you're familiar with the staff and the departments that you need to deal with. This can provide a feeling of comfort that takes much longer to develop in a large company. Departments are likely to be small and have close connections with each other, which helps to make internal communication work well – everyone knows what's going on. You'll also gain a better understanding of how your own role fits into the company as a whole.

In a small business you're likely to have considerable variety in your workload, including opportunities to work in different areas of the company, which will allow you to identify abilities that you didn't know you had. An introduction to new activities could even lead to a change of career. This variety in your work will help to make it stimulating, so you have a good reason for getting out of bed in the morning.

There will be plenty of opportunities to show initiative, and you'll also learn to function well as part of a team. Because it's much harder to overlook someone within a small workforce than a large one, your efforts are more likely to attract the attention of those higher up. You'll have plenty of opportunity to show what you can do, and to have your potential noticed. The result is very likely to be that promotion comes to you faster.

Small businesses are usually flexible, something that is rarely true of large organisations. This means that if they're well managed, they can adapt to make the most of changes in the wider economy, which in turn can help you. Don't dismiss them as a place to work because of the myths about them. Small firms can be ideal places for developing your career.

Questions 15–20

Complete the sentences below.

Choose **ONE WORD ONLY** *from the text for each answer.*

Write your answers in boxes 15–20 on your answer sheet.

15   In a small business it is easy to become .... with colleagues and other departments.

16   You may find you have .... you were not aware of.

17   Finding that your work is .... will make you enjoy doing it.

18   Other people are likely to realise that you have ....

19   Opportunities for .... will come sooner than in a larger business.

20   You can benefit from a small company being more .... than a large one.

Read the text below and answer Questions 21–27.

Starting a new job

A   Make sure you know when and where you are expected to report on your first day. If the route from home is unfamiliar to you, make a practice run first: the normal first activity in a new job is a meeting with your boss, and it would be embarrassing to be late. Dress formally until you're sure of the dress code.

B   You should expect to have an induction programme planned for you: a security pass; visits to whatever parts of the organisation you need to understand to do your job properly; meetings with anyone who could affect your success in the role; and someone to show you where everything is and tell you all the real rules of the culture – the ones that are never written down but which everyone is meant to follow.

C   It can be a shock to join a new organisation. When you are a newcomer, feeling uncertain and perhaps a little confused, there can be a strong temptation to talk about your old job and organisation as a way of reminding yourself and telling others that you really know what you are doing, because you did it in your previous role. Unfortunately, this will suggest that you have a high opinion of yourself, and that you think your old place was better. It has enormous power to annoy, so don't do it.

D   All employers have a core product or service paid for by customers which justifies their existence. If you are not part of this core activity, remember that your role is to provide a service to the people who *are* part of it. Understanding their concerns and passions is essential for understanding why your own role exists, and for knowing how to work alongside these colleagues. This is why you must see this product or service in action.

E   When I worked for a television company, all of us, whatever our job, were strongly encouraged to visit a studio and see how programmes were made. This was wise. Make sure you do the equivalent for whatever is the core activity of your new employer.

F   Don't try to do the job too soon. This may seem strange because, after all, you have been appointed to get on and do the job. But in your first few weeks your task is to learn what the job really is, rather than immediately starting to do what you assume it is.

G   Starting a new job is one of life's major transitions. Treat it with the attention it deserves and you will find that all your work in preparing and then going through the selection process has paid off magnificently.

Questions 21–27

The text on page 66 has seven paragraphs, **A–G**.

Which paragraph mentions the following?

*Write the correct letter, **A–G**, in boxes 21–27 on your answer sheet.*

NB *You may use any letter more than once.*

21 the emotions that new employees are likely to experience at first

22 a warning to be patient at first

23 how colleagues might react to certain behaviour

24 travelling to your new workplace before you start working there

25 an example of observing an activity carried out within an organisation

26 some things that the organisation should arrange for when you begin

27 a division of jobs within an organisation into two categories

SECTION 3   *Questions 28–40*

Read the text below and answer Questions 28–40.

How animals keep fit

No one would dream of running a marathon without first making a serious effort to train for it. But no matter how well they have stuck to their training regime, contestants will find that running non-stop for 42 kilometres is going to hurt.

Now consider the barnacle goose. Every year this bird carries out a 3000-kilometre migration. So how do the birds prepare for this? Do they spend months gradually building up fitness? That's not really the barnacle goose's style. Instead, says environmental physiologist Lewis Halsey, 'They just basically sit on the water and eat a lot.'

Until recently, nobody had really asked whether exercise is as tightly connected to fitness in the rest of the animal kingdom as it is for us. The question is tied up in a broader assumption: that animals maintain fitness because of the exercise they get finding food and escaping predators.

Halsey points out that this may not necessarily be the case. Take the house cat. Most domestic cats spend much of the day lounging around, apparently doing nothing, rather than hunting for food. But over short distances, even the laziest can move incredibly fast when they want to. Similarly, black and brown bears manage to come out of several months' hibernation with their muscle mass intact – without having to lift so much as a paw during this time.

Barnacle geese go one better. In the process of sitting around, they don't just maintain their fitness. They also develop stronger hearts and bigger flight muscles, enabling them to fly for thousands of kilometres in a migration that may last as little as two days.

So, if exercise isn't necessarily the key to physical strength, then what is? One clue comes from a broader view of the meaning of physical fitness. Biologically speaking, all it means is that the body has undergone changes that make it stronger and more efficient. In animals such as bears these changes appear to be triggered by cues such as falling temperatures or insufficient food. In the months of hibernation, these factors seem to prompt the release of muscle-protecting compounds which are then carried to the bears' muscles in their blood and prevent muscle loss.

Barnacle geese, Halsey suggests, may be responding to an environmental change such as temperature, which helps their bodies somehow 'know' that a big physical challenge is looming. In other bird species, that cue may be something different. Chris Guglielmo, a physiological ecologist, has studied the effect of subjecting migratory songbirds known as yellow-rumped warblers to changing hours of daylight. 'We don't need to take little songbirds and train them up to do a 6- or 10-hour flight,' he says. If they are subjected to the right daylight cycle, 'we can take them out of the cage and put them in the wind tunnel, and they fly for 10 hours.'

Unlike migratory birds, however, humans have no biological shortcut to getting fit. Instead, pressures in our evolutionary history made our bodies tie fitness to exercise.

Our ancestors' lives were unpredictable. They had to do a lot of running to catch food and escape danger, but they also needed to keep muscle mass to a minimum because muscle is biologically expensive. Each kilogram contributes about 10 to 15 kilocalories a day to our metabolism when resting – which doesn't sound like much until you realise that muscles account for about 40 percent of the average person's body mass. 'Most of us are spending 20 percent of our basic energy budget taking care of muscle mass,' says Daniel Lieberman, an evolutionary biologist and marathon runner.

So our physiology evolved to let our weight and fitness fluctuate depending on how much food was available. 'This makes us evolutionarily different from most other animals,' says Lieberman. In general, animals merely need to be capable of short bouts of intense activity, whether it's the cheetah chasing prey or the gazelle escaping. Cats are fast, but they don't need to run very far. Perhaps a few mad dashes around the house are all it takes to keep a domestic one fit enough for feline purposes. 'Humans, on the other hand, needed to adapt to run slower, but for longer,' says Lieberman.

He argues that long ago on the African savannah, natural selection made us into 'supremely adapted' endurance athletes, capable of running prey into the ground and ranging over long distances with unusual efficiency. But only, it appears, if we train. Otherwise we quickly degenerate into couch potatoes.

As for speed, even those animals that do cover impressive distances don't have to be the fastest they can possibly be. Barnacle geese needn't set world records when crossing the North Atlantic; they just need to be able to get to their destination. 'And,' says exercise physiologist Ross Tucker, 'humans may be the only animal that actually cares about reaching peak performance.' Other than racehorses and greyhounds, both of which we have bred to race, animals aren't directly competing against one another. 'I don't know that all animals are the same, performance-wise … and we don't know whether training would enhance their ability,' he says.

Questions 28–30

*Choose the correct letter, **A**, **B**, **C** or **D**.*

Write the correct letter in boxes 28–30 on your answer sheet.

28   The writer discusses marathon runners and barnacle geese to introduce the idea that

    A   marathon runners may be using inefficient training methods.
    B   the role of diet in achieving fitness has been underestimated.
    C   barnacle geese spend much longer preparing to face a challenge.
    D   serious training is not always necessary for physical achievement.

29   The writer says that human muscles

    A   use up a lot of energy even when resting.
    B   are heavier than other types of body tissue.
    C   were more efficiently used by our ancestors.
    D   have become weaker than they were in the past.

30   The writer says that in order to survive, early humans developed the ability to

    A   hide from their prey.
    B   run long distances.
    C   adapt their speeds to different situations.
    D   predict different types of animal movements.

Questions 31–35

Complete the summary below.

*Choose **ONE WORD ONLY** from the text for each answer.*

Write your answers in boxes 31–35 on your answer sheet.

What is the key to physical fitness?

In biological terms, when an animal is physically fit, its body changes, becoming more powerful and **31** .... For bears, this change may be initially caused by colder weather or a lack of **32** .... , which during **33** .... causes certain compounds to be released into their **34** .... and to travel around the body. These compounds appear to prevent muscle loss. In the case of barnacle geese, the change may be due to a variation in **35** ....

Questions 36–40

Look at the following statements (Questions 36–40) and the list of researchers below.

*Match each statement with the correct researcher, **A**, **B**, **C** or **D**.*

*Write the correct letter, **A**, **B**, **C** or **D**, in boxes 36–40 on your answer sheet.*

***NB** You may use any letter more than once.*

36 One belief about how animals stay fit is possibly untrue.

37 It may not be possible to train all animals to improve their speed.

38 One type of bird has demonstrated fitness when exposed to a stimulus in experimental conditions.

39 Human energy use developed in a different way from that of animals.

40 One type of bird may develop more strength when the weather becomes warmer or cooler.

List of Researchers

A   Lewis Halsey

B   Chris Guglielmo

C   Daniel Lieberman

D   Ross Tucker

WRITING TASK 1

You should spend about 20 minutes on this task.

A friend of yours is thinking about applying for the same course that you did at university. He/She has asked for your advice about studying this subject.

Write a letter to your friend. In your letter
- *give details of the course you took at the university*
- *explain why you recommend the university*
- *give some advice about how to apply*

Write at least 150 words.

You do **NOT** need to write any addresses.

Begin your letter as follows:

Dear .... ,

WRITING TASK 2

You should spend about 40 minutes on this task.

Write about the following topic:

In the future, more people will choose to go on holiday in their own country and not travel abroad on holiday.

Do you agree or disagree?

Give reasons for your answer and include any relevant examples from your own knowledge or experience.

Write at least 250 words.

SPEAKING

PART 1

The examiner asks the candidate about him/herself, his/her home, work or studies and other familiar topics.

EXAMPLE

Swimming

- Did you learn to swim when you were a child? [Why/Why not?]
- How often do you go swimming now? [Why/Why not?]
- What places are there for swimming where you live? [Why?]
- Do you think it would be more enjoyable to go swimming outdoors or at an indoor pool? [Why?]

PART 2

Describe a famous business person that you know about.

You should say:
    who this person is
    what kind of business this person is involved in
    what you know about this business person

and explain what you think of this business person.

You will have to talk about the topic for one to two minutes. You have one minute to think about what you are going to say. You can make some notes to help you if you wish.

PART 3

Discussion topics:

Famous people today

Example questions:
What kinds of people are most famous in your country today?
Why are there so many stories about famous people in the news?
Do you agree or disagree that many young people today want to be famous?

Advantages of being famous

Example questions:
Do you think it is easy for famous people to earn a lot of money?
Why might famous people enjoy having fans?
In what ways could famous people use their influence to do good things in the world?

Test 4

PART 1   *Questions 1–10*

Complete the form below.

Listening test audio

*Write **ONE WORD AND/OR A NUMBER** for each answer.*

Customer Satisfaction Survey

Customer details

Name:	Sophie Bird
Occupation:	**1** ....
Reason for travel today:	**2** ....

Journey information

Name of station returning to:	**3** ....
Type of ticket purchased:	standard **4** .... ticket
Cost of ticket:	**5** £ ....
When ticket was purchased:	yesterday
Where ticket was bought:	**6** ....

Satisfaction with journey

Most satisfied with:	the wifi
Least satisfied with:	the **7** .... this morning

Satisfaction with station facilities

Most satisfied with:	how much **8** .... was provided
Least satisfied with:	lack of seats, particularly on the **9** ....
Neither satisfied nor dissatisfied with:	the **10** .... available

---

PART 2   *Questions 11–20*

Questions 11–16

Label the map below.

*Write the correct letter, **A–H**, next to Questions 11–16.*

Listening test audio

Croft Valley Park

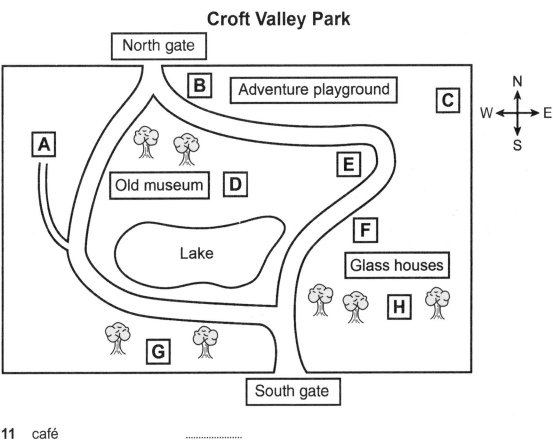

11	café	....
12	toilets	....
13	formal gardens	....
14	outdoor gym	....
15	skateboard ramp	....
16	wild flowers	....

Questions 17 and 18

Choose TWO letters, A–E.

What does the speaker say about the adventure playground?

- **A**   Children must be supervised.
- **B**   It costs more in winter.
- **C**   Some activities are only for younger children.
- **D**   No payment is required.
- **E**   It was recently expanded.

Questions 19 and 20

Choose TWO letters, A–E.

What does the speaker say about the glass houses?

- **A**   They are closed at weekends.
- **B**   Volunteers are needed to work there.
- **C**   They were badly damaged by fire.
- **D**   More money is needed to repair some of the glass.
- **E**   Visitors can see palm trees from tropical regions.

PART 3   *Questions 21–30*

Questions 21–24

*Choose the correct letter, **A**, **B** or **C**.*

Listening test audio

Presentation about refrigeration

21 What did Annie discover from reading about icehouses?

    A   why they were first created
    B   how the ice was kept frozen
    C   where they were located

22 What point does Annie make about refrigeration in ancient Rome?

    A   It became a commercial business.
    B   It used snow from nearby.
    C   It took a long time to become popular.

23 In connection with modern refrigerators, both Annie and Jack are worried about

    A   the complexity of the technology.
    B   the fact that some are disposed of irresponsibly.
    C   the large number that quickly break down.

24 What do Jack and Annie agree regarding domestic fridges?

    A   They are generally good value for money.
    B   There are plenty of useful variations.
    C   They are more useful than other domestic appliances.

Questions 25–30

Who is going to do research into each topic?

*Write the correct letter, **A**, **B** or **C**, next to Questions 25–30.*

People
A   Annie
B   Jack
C   both Annie and Jack

Topics

25   the goods that are refrigerated   ....

26   the effects on health   ....

27   the impact on food producers   ....

28   the impact on cities   ....

29   refrigerated transport   ....

30   domestic fridges   ....

PART 4   *Questions 31–40*

Complete the notes below.

*Write **ONE WORD ONLY** for each answer.*

Listening test audio

How the Industrial Revolution affected life in Britain

19th century

- For the first time, people's possessions were used to measure Britain's **31** ....

- Developments in production of goods and in **32** .... greatly changed lives.

MAIN AREAS OF CHANGE

Manufacturing

- The Industrial Revolution would not have happened without the new types of **33** .... that were used then.

- The leading industry was **34** .... (its products became widely available).

- New **35** .... made factories necessary and so more people moved into towns.

Transport

- The railways took the place of canals.

- Because of the new transport:

    - greater access to **36** .... made people more aware of what they could buy in shops.

    - when shopping, people were not limited to buying **37** .... goods.

Retailing

- The first department stores were opened.

- The displays of goods were more visible:

    - inside stores because of better **38** ....

    - outside stores, because **39** .... were bigger.

- **40** .... that was persuasive became much more common.

READING

SECTION 1　　*Questions 1–14*

Read the text below and answer Questions 1–7.

New cycle path to Marshbrook Country Park

A　A new dual-purpose cycle and pedestrian route has been built from Atherton bus station to the country park's main entrance at Marshbrook. It avoids the main road into Atherton on the south side, and keeps mainly to less busy roads. Once the path leaves the built-up area, it goes through countryside until it reaches Marshbrook.

B　Funding for the cycle path has come largely from the county and town councils, while almost a third of it was raised through crowdfunding. Maintenance of the path is the responsibility of the county council. The cycle path was completed ahead of schedule – partly thanks to perfect weather for construction – and under budget.

C　Annie Newcome is the chief executive of Cycle Atherton, the organisation that aims to get people cycling more often and more safely. Cycle Atherton proposed the 12-kilometre-long cycle path initially, and has been active in promoting it. Ms Newcome says she is delighted that all the hard work to achieve the funding proved successful.

D　Marshbrook Country Park is a very popular recreational area, and the new path makes it much easier to reach from the town in an environmentally friendly way. At 2.5 metres wide, it is also suitable for users of wheelchairs, mobility scooters and buggies, who have not previously had access to the park without using motor vehicles.

E　Although the path is now open, work is continuing to improve the signs along it, such as warnings when the path approaches a road. New hedges and trees will also be planted along stretches of the path, to provide some shelter from the wind and to benefit wildlife.

F　Further information and a detailed map of the path including a proposed 5-kilometre extension are available online. The map can easily be downloaded and printed. Visit the county council website and follow the links to Atherton Cycle Path.

Questions 1–7

The text on page 82 has six paragraphs, **A–F**.

Which paragraph mentions the following?

*Write the correct letter, **A–F**, in boxes 1–7 on your answer sheet.*

NB *You may use any letter more than once.*

1   what still needs to be done

2   the original suggestion for creating the path

3   a reason why the path opened early

4   people who no longer need to get to the park by car

5   the route of the path

6   the length of the path

7   who paid for the path

Read the text below and answer Questions 8–14.

Study dramatic arts at Thornley

If you are hoping for a career in the theatre, Thornley College of Dramatic Arts is the place to come. For fifty years we have been providing top-quality courses for actors, directors, producers, musicians and everyone else who wishes to work professionally in the theatre or related industries. We also have expertise in preparing students for the specialised requirements of TV, film and radio. We'll make sure you're thoroughly prepared for the reality of work in your chosen field.

Our college-based tutors all have extensive practical experience in the entertainment industry as well as academic qualifications, and we also collaborate with some of the country's best directors, writers and actors to create challenging, inspiring and exciting projects with our students.

We are well-known around the world, with our students coming from every continent. Every year, we receive two thousand applications for the one hundred places on our degree courses. Only the most talented get places, and we are proud that over ninety percent of our students gain professional work within a year of graduating – a figure few other drama colleges in the UK can match.

To mark our fiftieth anniversary this year, we are putting on a production of *Theatre 500*. Written by two staff members especially for this occasion, this multimedia show celebrates five hundred years of drama, and involves all our students in one way or another.

Another major development is that the college is about to move. Our new premises are now under construction in the heart of Thornley, next to the council building, which has won a prize for its architecture. For the last two years, we have been developing designs with Miller Furbank Architects for our new home, and one aim has been to ensure the buildings complement the council offices. Work started on the foundations of the buildings in March last year, and we plan to move to the new site this coming September.

We have also been talking to cultural organisations in the district, and considering how we can bring cost-free benefits to the local community, as well as to our students. As a result, part of the space in the new buildings has been designed to be adaptable, in order to accommodate classes, performances and workshops for different-sized groups of local people.

Questions 8–14

Do the following statements agree with the information given in the text on page 84?

In boxes 8–14 on your answer sheet, write

TRUE *if the statement agrees with the information*
FALSE *if the statement contradicts the information*
NOT GIVEN *if there is no information on this*

8   The college has introduced new courses since it opened.

9   The college provides training for work in the film industry.

10   Students have the chance to work with relevant professionals.

11   Many more people apply to study at the college than are accepted.

12   *Theatre 500* was created by students.

13   The new building and the council building were designed by the same architects.

14   Local groups will be charged for using college premises.

SECTION 2   *Questions 15–27*

Read the text below and answer Questions 15–20.

How to make your working day more enjoyable

Research shows that work takes up approximately a third of our lives. Most of us get so bogged down with day-to-day tasks though, that we easily forget why we originally applied for the job and what we can get out of it. Here are a few ideas for how to make your working day better.

Physical changes to your work environment can make a massive difference to how you feel. Get some green plants or a family photo for your desk. File all those odd bits of paper or throw them away. All of these little touches can make your work environment feel like it's yours. Make sure any screens you have are at a suitable height so you're not straining your neck and shoulders.

Humans need a change of environment every now and then to improve productivity. Go out at lunchtime for a quick walk. If you have the option, it's a good idea to work from home occasionally. And if there's a conference coming up, ask if you can go along to it. Not only will you practise your networking skills, but you'll also have a day away from the office.

Use coffee time to get to know a colleague you don't usually speak to. There's no point in getting away from staring at one thing though, only to replace it with another; so leave your mobile alone! Another tip is to try and stay out of office gossip. In the long run it could get you in more trouble than you realise.

When you're trying to focus on something, hunger is the worst thing. If you can, keep some healthy snacks in your desk because if you have something you can nibble on, it will make you work more effectively and you'll enjoy it more. Also, if you're dehydrated, you won't be able to focus properly. So keep drinking water.

Finally, if you've been dreaming about starting up a big project for some time, do it! There are so many different things you can do to get you enjoying work more each day.

Questions 15–20

Complete the sentences below.

*Choose **ONE WORD ONLY** from the text for each answer.*

Write your answers in boxes 15–20 on your answer sheet.

15   Bringing a personal .... to work will make the place feel more homely.

16   It is important to check the position of all .... before use to avoid pulling any muscles.

17   Leaving the office in the middle of the day may help to raise .... later on.

18   It is advisable to avoid checking a .... during breaks.

19   Getting involved in .... at work may have negative results.

20   Having a few .... available can help people concentrate better at work.

Read the text below and answer Questions 21–27.

How to get promoted

If you're sitting at your desk wondering whether this will be the year you finally get promoted, here are some tips.

It starts with you. You are perhaps the most important part in the 'promotion process', so you need to know what you want – and why you want it. Take an honest look at yourself – your achievements and also your skills, particularly those you could exploit to take on a different role.

Your boss is the gatekeeper. If you think your boss is likely to be on your side, ask for a meeting to discuss your serious commitment to the organisation and how this could translate into a more defined career plan. If you are less sure about your boss's view of your prospects and how they may react, start softly with a more deliberate focus on increasing your boss's understanding of the work you do and the added value you deliver.

Think about how you are perceived at work. In order for you to get your promotion, who needs to know about you? Who would be on the interview panel and whose opinion and input would they seek? And once you've got a list of people to impress, ask yourself – do they know enough about you? And I mean really know – what you do day to day at your desk, your contribution to the team, and perhaps most importantly, your potential.

The chances are that those decision-makers won't know all they should about you. Raising your profile in your organisation is critical so that when those in charge start looking at that empty office and considering how best to fill it, the first name that pops into their heads is yours. If your firm has a newsletter, volunteer to write a feature to include in it. If they arrange regular client events, get involved in the organisation of them. And so on.

If you think your experience needs enhancing, then look at ways you can continue to improve it. If you are confident in your professional expertise but lack the latest management theory, enrol on some relevant courses that fit around your day job.

So what are you waiting for?

Questions 21–27

Complete the notes below.

*Choose **ONE WORD ONLY** from the text for each answer.*

Write your answers in boxes 21–27 on your answer sheet.

Steps to take to achieve a promotion

- First step: examine past successes and any **21** .... that would help gain promotion

- Set up a meeting with your boss to talk about:

  - how best to use your high level of **22** .... in future

  - or how much extra **23** .... you already bring to the company

- Focus on the important people in the company:

  - find out which ones will be members of the **24** .... who decide on the promotion

  - consider how much they are aware of your **25** .... for the future

- Take steps to raise your profile by:

  - offering to create a feature for a company publication

  - participating in the **26** .... of events for customers

- Work on self-development:

  - take any **27** .... that fill in gaps in knowledge

→ 🔊 p. 128

SECTION 3   *Questions 28–40*

Read the text below and answer Questions 28–40.

Animals can tell right from wrong

Until recently, humans were thought to be the only species to experience complex emotions and have a sense of morality. But Professor Marc Bekoff, an ecologist at University of Colorado, Boulder, US, believes that morals are 'hard-wired' into the brains of all mammals and provide the 'social glue' that allows animals to live together in groups.

His conclusions will assist animal welfare groups pushing to have animals treated more humanely. Professor Bekoff, who presents his case in his book *Wild Justice*, said: 'Just as in humans, the moral nuances of a particular culture or group will be different from another, but they are certainly there. Moral codes are species specific, so they can be difficult to compare with each other or with humans.' Professor Bekoff believes morals developed in animals to help regulate behaviour in social groups. He claims that these help to limit fighting within the group and encourage co-operative behaviour.

His ideas have met with some controversy in the scientific community. Professor Frans de Waal, who examines the behaviour of primates, including chimpanzees, at Emory University, Atlanta, Georgia, US, said: 'I don't believe animals are moral in the sense we humans are – with a well-developed and reasoned sense of right and wrong – rather that human morality incorporates a set of psychological tendencies and capacities such as empathy, reciprocity, a desire for co-operation and harmony that are older than our species. Human morality was not formed from scratch, but grew out of our primate psychology. Primate psychology has ancient roots, and I agree that other animals show many of the same tendencies and have an intense sociality.'

Wolves live in tight-knit social groups that are regulated by strict rules. Wolves also demonstrate fairness. During play, dominant wolves will appear to exchange roles with lower-ranking wolves. They pretend to be submissive and go so far as to allow biting by the lower-ranking wolves, provided it is not too hard. Prof Bekoff argues that without a moral code governing their actions, this kind of behaviour would not be possible. Astonishingly, if an animal becomes aggressive, it will perform a 'play bow' to ask forgiveness before play resumes.

In other members of the dog family, play is controlled in a similar way. Among coyotes, cubs which are too aggressive are ignored by the rest of the group and often end up having to leave entirely. Experiments with domestic dogs, where one animal was given some 'sweets' and another wasn't, have shown that they possess a sense of fairness as they allowed their companion to eat some.

Elephants are intensely sociable and emotional animals. Research by Iain Douglas-Hamilton, from the department of zoology at Oxford University, suggests elephants experience compassion and has found evidence of elephants helping injured members of their herd. In 2003, a herd of 11 elephants rescued antelopes which were being held inside an enclosure in KwaZulu-Natal, South Africa. The top female elephant unfastened all of the metal latches holding the gates closed and swung them open, allowing the antelopes to escape. This is thought to be a rare example of animals showing empathy for members of another species – a trait previously thought to be the exclusive preserve of humankind.

A laboratory experiment involved training Diana monkeys to insert a token into a slot to obtain food. A male who had become skilled at the task was found to be helping the oldest female, who had not learned how to do it. On three occasions the male monkey picked up tokens she dropped and inserted them into the slot and allowed her to have the food. As there was no benefit for the male monkey, Professor Bekoff argues that this is a clear example of an animal's actions being driven by some internal moral compass.

Since chimpanzees are known to be among the most cognitively advanced of the great apes and our closest cousins, it is perhaps not remarkable that scientists should suggest they live by moral codes. A chimpanzee known as Knuckles is the only known captive chimpanzee to suffer from cerebral palsy, which leaves him physically and mentally impaired. What is extraordinary is that scientists have observed other chimpanzees interacting with him differently and he is rarely subjected to intimidating displays of aggression from older males. Chimpanzees also demonstrate a sense of justice and those who deviate from the code of conduct of a group are set upon by other members as punishment.

Experiments with rats have shown that they will not take food if they know their actions will cause pain to another rat. In lab tests, rats were given food which then caused a second group of rats to receive an electric shock. The rats with the food stopped eating rather than see this happen.

Whales have been found to have spindle cells in their brains. These specialised cells were thought to be restricted to humans and great apes, and appear to play a role in empathy and understanding the emotions of others. Humpback whales, fin whales, killer whales and sperm whales have all been found to have spindle cells. They also have three times as many spindle cells as humans and are thought to be older in evolutionary terms. This finding suggests that emotional judgements such as empathy may have evolved considerably earlier in history than formerly thought and could be widespread in the animal kingdom.

Questions 28–32

Complete the summary below.

Choose **ONE WORD ONLY** *from the text for each answer.*

Write your answers in boxes 28–32 on your answer sheet.

Complex social behaviour in wolf packs

Wolves live in packs and it is clear that there are a number of **28** ....
concerning their behaviour. Some observers believe they exhibit a sense of
29 .... the stronger, more senior wolves seem to adopt the roles
of the junior wolves when they are playing together. They act as if they are
30 .... to the juniors and even permit some gentle
31 .... What is even more surprising is that when one of the juniors
gets too forceful, it bends down begging for **32** .... Only when that
has been granted will the wolves continue playing.

Questions 33–37

Look at the following animals (Questions 33–37) and the list of descriptions below.

*Match each animal with the correct description, **A–G**.*

*Write the correct letter, **A–G**, in boxes 33–37 on your answer sheet.*

33   coyotes

34   domestic dogs

35   elephants

36   Diana monkeys

37   rats

List of Descriptions

A   often attack peers who fail to follow the moral code

B   appear to enjoy playing with members of a different species

C   sometimes share treats with a peer

D   may assist a peer who is failing to complete a task

E   may be driven away by their peers if they do not obey the moral code

F   seem unwilling to benefit from something that hurts their peers

G   may help a different type of animal which is in difficulty

---

Questions 38–40

Choose the correct letter, A, B, C or D.

Write the correct letter in boxes 38–40 on your answer sheet.

38   What view is expressed by Professor de Waal?

    A   Apes have advanced ideas about the difference between good and evil.
    B   The social manners of some animals prove that they are highly moral.
    C   Some human moral beliefs developed from our animal ancestors.
    D   The desire to live in peace with others is a purely human quality.

39   Why does Professor Bekoff mention the experiment on Diana monkeys?

    A   It shows that this species of monkey is not very easy to train.
    B   It confirms his view on the value of research into certain monkeys.
    C   It proves that female monkeys are generally less intelligent than males.
    D   It illustrates a point he wants to make about monkeys and other creatures.

40   What does the writer find most surprising about chimpanzees?

    A   They can suffer from some of the same illnesses as humans.
    B   They appear to treat disabled peers with consideration.
    C   They have sets of social conventions that they follow.
    D   The males can be quite destructive at times.

WRITING TASK 1

You should spend about 20 minutes on this task.

> *You have seen an advertisement from a couple, who live in Australia, for someone to teach their two children your language for a year.*
>
> *Write a letter to the couple. In your letter*
> - *explain why you think you would be suitable for the job*
> - *say what else you could do for the family*
> - *give your reasons for wanting the job*

Write at least 150 words.

You do **NOT** need to write any addresses.

Begin your letter as follows:

Dear .... ,

WRITING TASK 2

You should spend about 40 minutes on this task.

Write about the following topic:

> **In many countries, paying for things using mobile phone (cellphone) apps is becoming increasingly common.**
>
> **Does this development have more advantages or more disadvantages?**

Give reasons for your answer and include any relevant examples from your own knowledge or experience.

Write at least 250 words.

PART 1

The examiner asks the candidate about him/herself, his/her home, work or studies and other familiar topics.

EXAMPLE

Jewellery

- How often do you wear jewellery? [Why/Why not?]
- What type of jewellery do you like best? [Why/Why not?]
- When do people like to give jewellery in your country [Why?]
- Have you ever given jewellery to someone as a gift? [Why/Why not?]

PART 2

> **Describe an interesting TV programme you watched about a science topic.**
>
> **You should say:**
> **what science topic this TV programme was about**
> **when you saw this TV programme**
> **what you learnt from this TV programme about a science topic**
>
> **and explain why you found this TV programme interesting.**

You will have to talk about the topic for one to two minutes. You have one minute to think about what you are going to say. You can make some notes to help you if you wish.

PART 3

Discussion topics:

Science and the public

Example questions:
How interested are most people in your country in science?
Why do you think children today might be better at science than their parents?
How do you suggest the public can learn more about scientific developments?

Scientific discoveries

Example questions:
What do you think are the most important scientific discoveries in the last 100 years?
Do you agree or disagree that there are no more major scientific discoveries left to make?
Who should pay for scientific research – governments or private companies?

Audioscripts

PART 1

AMBER:	Hello William. This is Amber – you said to phone if I wanted to get more information about the job agency you mentioned. Is now a good time?
WILLIAM:	Oh, hi Amber. Yes. Fine. So the agency I was talking about is called Bankside – they're based in Docklands – I can tell you the address now – 497 Eastside.
AMBER:	OK, thanks. So is there anyone in particular I should speak to there?
WILLIAM:	The agent I always deal with is called Becky Jamieson.
AMBER:	Let me write that down – Becky …
WILLIAM:	Jamieson J-A-M-I-E-S-O-N.

Q1

AMBER:	Do you have her direct line?
WILLIAM:	Yes, it's in my contacts somewhere – right, here we are: 078 double 6, 510 triple 3. I wouldn't call her until the afternoon if I were you – she's always really busy in the morning trying to fill last-minute vacancies. She's really helpful and friendly so I'm sure it would be worth getting in touch with her for an informal chat.

Q2

AMBER:	It's mainly clerical and admin jobs they deal with, isn't it?
WILLIAM:	That's right. I know you're hoping to find a full-time job in the media eventually – but Becky mostly recruits temporary staff for the finance sector – which will look good on your CV – and generally pays better too.
AMBER:	Yeah – I'm just a bit worried because I don't have much office experience.
WILLIAM:	I wouldn't worry. They'll probably start you as a receptionist, or something like that. So what's important for that kind of job isn't so much having business skills or knowing lots of different computer systems – it's communication that really matters – so you'd be fine there. And you'll pick up office skills really quickly on the job. It's not that complicated.

Q3

AMBER:	OK good. So how long do people generally need temporary staff for? It would be great if I could get something lasting at least a month.
WILLIAM:	That shouldn't be too difficult. But you're more likely to be offered something for a week at first, which might get extended. It's unusual to be sent somewhere for just a day or two.

Q4

AMBER:	Right. I've heard the pay isn't too bad – better than working in a shop or a restaurant.
WILLIAM:	Oh yes – definitely. The hourly rate is about £10, 11 if you're lucky.

Q5

AMBER:	That's pretty good. I was only expecting to get eight or nine pounds an hour.

WILLIAM:	Do you want me to tell you anything about the registration process?
AMBER:	Yes, please. I know you have to have an interview.
WILLIAM:	The interview usually takes about an hour and you should arrange that about a week in advance.
AMBER:	I suppose I should dress smartly if it's for office work – I can probably borrow a suit from Mum.

Q6

WILLIAM:	Good idea. It's better to look too smart than too casual.
AMBER:	Will I need to bring copies of my exam certificates or anything like that?
WILLIAM:	No – they don't need to see those, I don't think.

AMBER:	What about my <u>passport</u>?	Q7
WILLIAM:	Oh yes – they will ask to see that.	
AMBER:	OK.	
WILLIAM:	I wouldn't get stressed about the interview though. It's just a chance for them to build a relationship with you – so they can try and match you to a job which you'll like. So there are questions about <u>personality</u> that they always ask candidates – fairly basic ones. And they probably won't ask anything too difficult like what your plans are for the future.	Q8
AMBER:	Hope not.	
WILLIAM:	Anyway, there are lots of benefits to using an agency – for example, the interview will be useful because they'll give you <u>feedback</u> on your performance so you can improve next time.	Q9
AMBER:	And they'll have access to jobs which aren't advertised.	
WILLIAM:	Exactly – most temporary jobs aren't advertised.	
AMBER:	And I expect finding a temporary job this way takes a lot less <u>time</u> – it's much easier than ringing up individual companies.	Q10
WILLIAM:	Yes indeed. Well I think …	

PART 2

Good morning. My name's Erica Matthews, and I'm the owner of Matthews Island Holidays, a company set up by my parents. Thank you for coming to this presentation, in which I hope to interest you in what we have to offer. We're a small, family-run company, and we believe in the importance of the personal touch, so we don't aim to compete with other companies on the number of customers. What we do is build on our <u>many years' experience – more than almost any other rail holiday company</u> – to ensure we provide perfect holidays in a small number of destinations, which we've got to know extremely well.

Q11

I'll start with our six-day Isle of Man holiday. This is a fascinating island in the Irish Sea, with Wales to the south, England to the east, Scotland to the north and Northern Ireland to the west. Our holiday starts in <u>Heysham, where your tour manager will meet you</u>, then you'll travel by ferry to the Isle of Man. Some people prefer to fly from Luton instead, and another popular option is to go by train to Liverpool and take a ferry from there.

Q12

You have five nights in the hotel, and the price covers five breakfasts and dinners, and <u>lunch on the three days when there are organised trips</u>: day four is free, and most people have lunch in a café or restaurant in Douglas.

Q13

The price of the holiday includes the ferry to the Isle of Man, all travel on the island, the hotel, and the meals I've mentioned. Incidentally, we try to make booking our holidays as simple and fair as possible, so unlike with many companies, the price is the same whether you book six months in advance or at the last minute, and there's no supplement for single rooms in hotels. <u>If you make a booking then need to change the start date, for example because of illness, you're welcome to change to an alternative date or a different tour, for a small administrative fee.</u>

Q14

OK, so what does the holiday consist of? Well, on day one you'll arrive in time for a short introduction by your tour manager, followed by dinner in the hotel. The dining room looks out at the <u>river</u>, close to where it flows into the harbour, and there's usually plenty of activity going on.

Q15

On day two you'll take the coach to the small town of Peel, on the way calling in at the Tynwald Exhibition. The Isle of Man isn't part of the United Kingdom, and it has its own parliament, called Tynwald. It's claimed that this is the world's oldest parliament that's still functioning, and that it dates back to 979. However, the earliest surviving reference to it is from <u>1422</u>, so perhaps it isn't quite as old as it claims!   Q16

Day three we have a trip to the mountain Snaefell. This begins with a leisurely ride along the promenade in Douglas in a horse-drawn tram. Then you board an electric train which takes you to the fishing village of Laxey. From there it's an eight-kilometre ride in the Snaefell Mountain Railway to the <u>top</u>. Lunch will be in the café, giving you spectacular views of the island.   Q17

Day four is free for you to explore, using the <u>pass</u> which we'll give you. So you won't have to   Q18
pay for travel on local transport, or for entrance to the island's heritage sites. Or you might just want to take it easy in Douglas and perhaps do a little light shopping.

The last full day, day five, is for some people the highlight of the holiday, with a ride on the <u>steam</u> railway, from Douglas to Port Erin. After some time to explore, a coach will take   Q19
you to the headland that overlooks the Calf of Man, a small island just off the coast. From there you continue to Castletown, which used to be the <u>capital</u> of the Isle of Man, and its   Q20
mediaeval castle.

And on day six it's back to the ferry – or the airport, if you flew to the island – and time to go home.

Now I'd like to tell you ...

PART 3

RUTH:	Ed, how are you getting on with the reading for our presentation next week?
ED:	Well, OK, Ruth – but there's so much of it.
RUTH:	I know, I hadn't realised birth order was such a popular area of research.
ED:	But the stuff on birth order and personality is mostly unreliable. From what I've been reading a lot of the claims about how your position in the family determines certain personality traits are just stereotypes, with no robust evidence to support them.
RUTH:	OK, but that's an interesting point – we could start by outlining what previous research has shown. There are studies going back over a hundred years.
ED:	Yeah – so we could just run through some of the typical traits. Like the consensus seems to be that oldest children are generally less well-adjusted because they never get over the arrival of a younger sibling.

RUTH: Right, but on a positive note, some studies claimed that <u>they were thought to</u>   Q21
<u>be good at nurturing – certainly in the past when people had large families they</u>
<u>would have been expected to look after the younger ones.</u>

ED: There isn't such a clear picture for middle children – but one trait that a lot of the studies mention is that they are easier to get on with than older or younger siblings.

RUTH: <u>Generally eager to please and helpful</u> – although that's certainly not accurate as   Q22
far as my family goes – my middle brother was a nightmare – always causing fights and envious of whatever I had.

ED: As I said – none of this seems to relate to my own experience. I'm the youngest in my family and I don't recognise myself in any of the studies I've read about. I'm supposed to have been <u>a sociable and confident child who made friends easily</u> –   Q23
but I was actually terribly shy.

RUTH: Really? That's funny. There have been hundreds of studies on twins but mostly about nurture versus nature …

ED:	There was one on personality, which said that a twin is likely to be <u>quite shy in social situations</u> because they always have their twin around to depend on for support.	Q24
RUTH:	My cousins were like that when they were small – they were only interested in each other and found it hard to engage with other kids. They're fine now though.	
ED:	Only children have had a really bad press – a lot of studies have branded them as <u>loners who think the world revolves around them</u> because they've never had to fight for their parents' attention.	Q25
RUTH:	That does seem a bit harsh. One category I hadn't considered before was children with much older siblings – a couple of studies mentioned that these children <u>grow up more quickly and are expected to do basic things for themselves – like getting dressed.</u>	Q26
ED:	I can see how that might be true – although I expect they're sometimes the exact opposite – playing the baby role and clamouring for special treatment.	

RUTH:	What was the problem with most of these studies, do you think?	
ED:	I think it was because in a lot of cases data was collected from only one sibling per family, who rated him or herself and his or her siblings at the same time.	
RUTH:	Mmm. Some of the old research into the relationship between birth order and academic achievement has been proved to be accurate though. Performances in intelligence tests decline slightly from the eldest child to his or her younger siblings. This has been proved in lots of recent studies.	
ED:	Yes. <u>Although what many of them didn't take into consideration was family size.</u> The more siblings there are, the likelier the family is to have a low socio-economic status – which can also account for differences between siblings in academic performance.	Q27
RUTH:	The oldest boy might be given more opportunities than his younger sisters, for example.	
ED:	Exactly.	
RUTH:	But the main reason for the marginally higher academic performance of oldest children is quite surprising, I think. It's not only that they benefit intellectually from extra attention at a young age – which is what I would have expected. <u>It's that they benefit from being teachers for their younger siblings, by verbalising processes.</u>	Q28
ED:	Right, and this gives them status and confidence, which again contribute, in a small way, to better performance. So would you say sibling rivalry has been a useful thing for you?	
RUTH:	I think so – my younger brother was incredibly annoying and we fought a lot but I think this has made me a stronger person. <u>I know how to defend myself</u>. We had some terrible arguments and I would have died rather than apologise to him – but <u>we had to put up with each other</u> and most of the time we co-existed amicably enough.	Q29/Q30 / Q29/Q30
ED:	Yes, my situation was pretty similar. But I don't think having two older brothers made me any less selfish – I was never prepared to let my brothers use any of my stuff …	
RUTH:	That's perfectly normal, whereas …	

PART 4

Today I'm going to talk about the eucalyptus tree. This is a very common tree here in Australia, where it's also sometimes called the gum tree. First I'm going to talk about why it's important, then I'm going to describe some problems it faces at present.

Right, well the eucalyptus tree is an important tree for lots of reasons. For example, it gives
shelter to creatures like birds and bats, and these and other species also depend on it for   *Q31*
food, particularly the nectar from its flowers. So it supports biodiversity. It's useful to us
humans too, because we can kill germs with a disinfectant made from oil extracted from   *Q32*
eucalyptus leaves.

The eucalyptus grows all over Australia and the trees can live for up to four hundred years.
So it's alarming that all across the country, numbers of eucalyptus are falling because the
trees are dying off prematurely. So what are the reasons for this?

One possible reason is disease. As far back as the 1970s the trees started getting a disease
called Mundulla Yellows. The trees' leaves would gradually turn yellow, then the tree would
die. It wasn't until 2004 that they found the cause of the problem was lime, or calcium
hydroxide to give it its proper chemical name, which was being used in the construction
of roads. The lime was being washed away into the ground and affecting the roots of the   *Q33*
eucalyptus trees nearby. What it was doing was preventing the trees from sucking up the iron
they needed for healthy growth. When this was injected back into the affected trees, they
immediately recovered.

But this problem only affected a relatively small number of trees. By 2000, huge numbers
of eucalyptus were dying along Australia's East Coast, of a disease known as Bell-miner
Associated Die-back. The bell-miner is a bird, and the disease seems to be common where
there are high populations of bell-miners. Again it's the leaves of the trees that are affected.
What happens is that insects settle on the leaves and eat their way round them, destroying   *Q34*
them as they go, and at the same time they secrete a solution which has sugar in it. The bell-
miner birds really like this solution, and in order to get as much as possible, they keep away
other creatures that might try to get it. So these birds and insects flourish at the expense of
other species, and eventually so much damage is done to the leaves that the tree dies.

But experts say that trees can start looking sick before any sign of Bell-miner Associated Die-
back. So it looks as if the problem might have another explanation. One possibility is that it's
to do with the huge bushfires that we have in Australia. A theory proposed over 40 years ago
by ecologist William Jackson is that the *frequency* of bushfires in a particular region affects
the type of vegetation that grows there. If there are very frequent bushfires in a region, this
encourages grass to grow afterwards, while if the bushfires are rather less frequent, this   *Q35*
results in the growth of eucalyptus forests.

So why is this? Why do fairly frequent bushfires actually support the growth of eucalyptus?
Well, one reason is that the fire stops the growth of other species which would consume
water needed by eucalyptus trees. And there's another reason. If these other quick-growing   *Q36*
species of bushes and plants are allowed to proliferate, they harm the eucalyptus in another
way, by affecting the composition of the soil, and removing nutrients from it. So some   *Q37*
bushfires are actually essential for the eucalyptus to survive as long as they are not too
frequent. In fact there's evidence that Australia's indigenous people practised regular burning
of bush land for thousands of years before the arrival of the Europeans.

But since Europeans arrived on the continent, the number of bushfires has been strictly
controlled. Now scientists believe that this reduced frequency of bushfires to low levels has
led to what's known as 'dry rainforest', which seems an odd name as usually we associate   *Q38*
tropical rainforest with wet conditions. And what's special about this type of rainforest? Well,
unlike tropical rainforest which is a rich ecosystem, this type of ecosystem is usually a simple   *Q39*
one. It has very thick, dense vegetation, but not much variety of species. The vegetation
provides lots of shade, so one species that does find it ideal is the bell-miner bird, which
builds its nests in the undergrowth there. But again that's not helpful for the eucalyptus tree.   *Q40*

TEST 2

PART 1

TIM: Good morning. You're through to the tourist information office, Tim speaking. How can I help you?

JEAN: Oh hello. Could you give me some information about next month's festival, please? My family and I will be staying in the town that week.

TIM: Of course. Well it starts with a concert on the afternoon of the 17th.

JEAN: Oh I heard about that. The orchestra and singers come from the USA, don't they?

TIM: They're from Canada. They're very popular over there. They're going to perform a number of well-known pieces that will appeal to children as well as adults.

JEAN: That sounds good. My whole family are interested in music.

TIM: The next day, the 18th, there's a performance by a ballet company called Eustatis.   *Q1*

JEAN: Sorry?

TIM: The name is spelt E-U-S-T-A-T-I-S. They appeared in last year's festival, and went down very well. Again, their programme is designed for all ages.

JEAN: Good. I expect we'll go to that. I hope there's going to be a play during the festival, a comedy, ideally.

TIM: You're in luck! On the 19th and 20th a local amateur group are performing one written by a member of the group. It's called *Jemima*. That'll be on in the town hall. They've already performed it two or three times. I haven't seen it myself, but the review in the local paper was very good.   *Q2*

JEAN: And is it suitable for children?

TIM: Yes, in fact it's aimed more at children than at adults, so both performances are in the afternoon.

JEAN: And what about dance? Will there be any performances?   *Q3*

TIM: Yes, also on the 20th, but in the evening. A professional company is putting on a show of modern pieces, with electronic music by young composers.

JEAN: Uh-huh.

TIM: The show is about how people communicate, or fail to communicate, with each other, so it's got the rather strange name, *Chat*.   *Q4*

JEAN: I suppose that's because that's something we do both face to face and online.

TIM: That's right.

TIM: Now there are also some workshops and other activities. They'll all take place at least once every day, so everyone who wants to take part will have a chance.

JEAN: Good. We're particularly interested in cookery – you don't happen to have a cookery workshop, do you?

TIM: We certainly do. It's going to focus on how to make food part of a healthy lifestyle, and it'll show that even sweet things like cakes can contain much less sugar than they usually do.   *Q5*

JEAN: That might be worth going to. We're trying to encourage our children to cook.

TIM: Another workshop is just for children, and that's on creating posters to reflect the history of the town. The aim is to make children aware of how both the town and people's lives have changed over the centuries. The results will be exhibited in the community centre. Then the other workshop is in toy-making, and that's for adults only.   *Q6*

JEAN:	Oh, why's that?	
TIM:	Because it involves carpentry – participants will be making toys out of <u>wood</u>, so there'll be a lot of sharp chisels and other tools around.	Q7
JEAN:	It makes sense to keep children away from it.	
TIM:	Exactly. Now let me tell you about some of the outdoor activities. There'll be supervised wild swimming …	
JEAN:	Wild swimming? What's that?	
TIM:	It just means swimming in natural waters, rather than a swimming pool.	
JEAN:	Oh OK. In a <u>lake</u>, for instance.	Q8
TIM:	Yes, there's a beautiful one just outside the town, and that'll be the venue for the swimming. There'll be lifeguards on duty, so it's suitable for all ages. And finally, there'll be a walk in some nearby woods every day. The leader is an expert on <u>insects</u>. He'll show some that live in the woods, and how important they are for the environment. So there are going to be all sorts of different things to do during the festival.	Q9
JEAN:	There certainly are.	
TIM:	If you'd like to read about how the preparations for the festival are going, the festival organiser is keeping a <u>blog</u>. Just search online for the festival website, and you'll find it.	Q10
JEAN:	Well, thank you very much for all the information.	
TIM:	You're welcome. Goodbye.	
JEAN:	Goodbye.	

PART 2

WOMAN:	I'm very pleased to welcome this evening's guest speaker, Mark Logan, who's going to tell us about the recent transformation of Minster Park. Over to you, Mark.	
MARK:	Thank you. I'm sure you're all familiar with Minster Park. It's been a feature of the city for well over a century, and has been the responsibility of the city council for most of that time. What perhaps isn't so well known is the origin of the park: <u>unlike many public parks that started in private ownership, as the garden of a large house, for instance, Minster was some waste land, which people living nearby started planting with flowers in 1892.</u> It was unclear who actually owned the land, and this wasn't settled until 20 years later, when the council took possession of it.	Q11
	You may have noticed the statue near one of the entrances. It's of Diane Gosforth, who played a key role in the history of the park. Once the council had become the legal owner, it planned to sell the land for housing. <u>Many local people</u> wanted it to remain a place that everyone could go to, to enjoy the fresh air and natural environment – remember the park is in a densely populated residential area. <u>Diane Gosforth was one of those people, and she organised petitions and demonstrations</u>, which eventually made the council change its mind about the future of the land.	Q12
	Soon after this the First World War broke out, in 1914, and most of the park was dug up and <u>planted with vegetables</u>, which were sold locally. At one stage the army considered taking it over for troop exercises and got as far as contacting the city council, then decided the park was too small to be of use. There were occasional public meetings during the war, in an area that had been retained as grass.	Q13

After the war, the park was turned back more or less to how it had been before 1914, and continued almost unchanged until recently. Plans for transforming it were drawn up at various times, most recently in 2013, though they were revised in 2015, before any work had started. <u>The changes finally got going in 2016</u>, and were finished on schedule last year.

Q14

OK, let me tell you about some of the changes that have been made – and some things that have been retained. If you look at this map, you'll see the familiar outline of the park, with the river forming the northern boundary, and a gate in each of the other three walls. The statue of Diane Gosforth has been moved: it used to be close to the south gate, but it's now <u>immediately to the north of the lily pond, almost in the centre of the park</u>, which makes it much more visible.

Q15

There's a new area of wooden sculptures, which are <u>on the river bank, where the path from the east gate makes a sharp bend</u>.

Q16

There are two areas that are particularly intended for children. The playground has been enlarged and improved, and that's <u>between the river and the path that leads from the pond to the river</u>.

Q17

Then there's a new maze, a circular series of paths, separated by low hedges. That's <u>near the west gate – you go north from there towards the river and then turn left to reach it</u>.

Q18

There have been tennis courts in the park for many years, and they've been doubled, from four to eight. They're still <u>in the south-west corner of the park, where there's a right-angle bend in the path</u>.

Q19

Something else I'd like to mention is the new fitness area. This is <u>right next to the lily pond on the same side as the west gate</u>.

Q20

Now, as you're all gardeners, I'm sure you'll like to hear about the plants that have been chosen for the park.

PART 3

CATHY:	OK, Graham, so let's check we both know what we're supposed to be doing.
GRAHAM:	OK.
CATHY:	So, for the university's open day, we have to plan a display on British life and literature in the mid-19th century.
GRAHAM:	That's right. But we'll have some people to help us find the materials and set it up, remember – for the moment, we just need to plan it.
CATHY:	Good. So have you gathered who's expected to come and see the display? Is it for the people studying English, or students from other departments? I'm not clear about it.
GRAHAM:	Nor me. That was how it used to be, but it didn't attract many people, so this year it's going to be part of an open day, to raise the university's profile. <u>It'll be publicised in the city, to encourage people to come and find out something of what goes on here.</u> And it's included in the information that's sent to <u>people who are considering applying to study here next year.</u>
CATHY:	Presumably some current students and lecturers will come?
GRAHAM:	I would imagine so, but we've been told to concentrate on the other categories of people.
CATHY:	Right. We don't have to cover the whole range of 19th-century literature, do we?

Q21/Q22

Q21/Q22

GRAHAM:	No, it's entirely up to us. I suggest just using Charles Dickens.	
CATHY:	That's a good idea. <u>Most people have heard of him, and have probably read some of his novels, or seen films based on them</u>, so that's a good lead-in to life in his time.	*Q23/Q24*
GRAHAM:	Exactly. <u>And his novels show the awful conditions that most people had to live in, don't they: he wanted to shock people into doing something about it</u>.	*Q23/Q24*
CATHY:	Did he do any campaigning, other than writing?	
GRAHAM:	Yes, he campaigned for education and other social reforms, and gave talks, but I'm inclined to ignore that and focus on the novels.	
CATHY:	Yes, I agree.	

CATHY:	OK, so now shall we think about a topic linked to each novel?	
GRAHAM:	Yes. I've printed out a list of Dickens's novels in the order they were published, in the hope you'd agree to focus on him!	
CATHY:	You're lucky I *did* agree! Let's have a look. OK, the first was *The Pickwick Papers*, published in 1836. It was very successful when it came out, wasn't it, and was adapted for the theatre straight away.	
GRAHAM:	There's an interesting point, though, that there's <u>a character who keeps falling asleep, and that medical condition was named after the book – Pickwickian Syndrome</u>.	*Q25*
CATHY:	Oh, so why don't we use that as the topic, and include some quotations from the novel?	
GRAHAM:	Right. Next is *Oliver Twist*. There's a lot in the novel about poverty. But maybe something less obvious …	
CATHY:	Well Oliver is taught how to steal, isn't he? We could use that to illustrate the fact that <u>very few children went to school, particularly not poor children, so they learnt in other ways</u>.	*Q26*
GRAHAM:	Good idea. What's next?	
CATHY:	Maybe *Nicholas Nickleby*. Actually he taught in a really cruel school, didn't he?	
GRAHAM:	That's right. But there's also the <u>company of touring actors that Nicholas joins. We could do something on theatres and other amusements of the time</u>. We don't want *only* the bad things, do we?	*Q27*
CATHY:	OK.	
GRAHAM:	What about *Martin Chuzzlewit*? He goes to the USA, doesn't he?	
CATHY:	Yes, and <u>Dickens himself had been there a year before, and drew on his experience there in the novel</u>.	*Q28*
GRAHAM:	I wonder, though … The main theme is selfishness, so we could do something on social justice? No, too general, let's keep to your idea – I think it would work well.	
CATHY:	He wrote *Bleak House* next – that's my favourite of his novels.	
GRAHAM:	Yes, mine too. His satire of the legal system is pretty powerful.	
CATHY:	That's true, but think about Esther, <u>the heroine. As a child she lives with someone she doesn't know is her aunt, who treats her very badly. Then she's very happy living with her guardian, and he puts her in charge of the household. And at the end she gets married and her guardian gives her and her husband a house, where of course they're very happy</u>.	*Q29*
GRAHAM:	Yes, I like that.	
CATHY:	What shall we take next? *Little Dorrit*? Old Mr Dorrit has been in a debtors' prison for years …	
GRAHAM:	So was Dickens's father, wasn't he?	
CATHY:	That's right.	

GRAHAM: What about focusing on <u>the part when Mr Dorrit inherits a fortune, and he starts pretending he's always been rich</u>?   *Q30*

CATHY: Good idea.

GRAHAM: OK, so next we need to think about what materials we want to illustrate each issue. That's going to be quite hard.

PART 4

I'm going to report on a case study of a programme which has been set up to help rural populations in Mozambique, a largely agricultural country in South-East Africa.

The programme worked with three communities in Chicualacuala district, near the Limpopo River. This is a dry and arid region, with unpredictable rainfall. Because of this, people in the area were unable to support themselves through agriculture and instead they used the forest as a means of providing themselves with an income, mainly by selling charcoal. However, this was not a sustainable way of living in the long term, as they were rapidly using up this resource.

To support agriculture in this dry region, the programme focused primarily on making use of existing water resources from the Limpopo River by setting up systems of <u>irrigation</u>, which   *Q31* would provide a dependable water supply for crops and animals. The programme worked closely with the district government in order to find the best way of implementing this. The region already had one farmers' association, and it was decided to set up two more of these. These associations planned and carried out activities including water management, livestock breeding and agriculture, and it was notable that in general, <u>women</u> formed the majority of   *Q32* the workforce.

It was decided that in order to keep the crops safe from animals, both wild and domestic, special areas should be fenced off where the crops could be grown. The community was responsible for creating these fences, but the programme provided the necessary <u>wire</u> for   *Q33* making them.

Once the area had been fenced off, it could be cultivated. The land was dug, so that vegetables and cereals appropriate to the climate could be grown, and the programme provided the necessary <u>seeds</u> for this. The programme also provided pumps so that water   *Q34* could be brought from the river in pipes to the fields. However, the labour was all provided by local people, and they also provided and put up the <u>posts</u> that supported the fences around   *Q35* the fields.

Once the programme had been set up, its development was monitored carefully. The farmers were able to grow enough produce not just for their own needs, but also to sell. However, getting the produce to places where it could be marketed was sometimes a problem, as the farmers did not have access to <u>transport</u>, and this resulted in large amounts of produce,   *Q36* especially vegetables, being spoiled. This problem was discussed with the farmers' associations and it was decided that in order to prevent food from being spoiled, the farmers needed to learn techniques for its <u>preservation</u>.   *Q37*

There was also an additional initiative that had not been originally planned, but which became a central feature of the programme. This was when farmers started to dig holes for tanks in the fenced-off areas and to fill these with water and use them for breeding <u>fish</u> – an important   *Q38* source of protein. After a time, another suggestion was made by local people which hadn't been part of the programme's original proposal, but which was also adopted later on. They decided to try setting up colonies of <u>bees</u>, which would provide honey both for their own   *Q39* consumption and to sell.

So what lessons can be learned from this programme? First of all, it tells us that in dry, arid regions, if there is access to a reliable source of water, there is great potential for the development of agriculture. In Chicualacuala, there was a marked improvement in agricultural production, which improved food security and benefited local people by providing them with both food and income. However, it's important to set realistic timelines for each phase of the programme, especially for its <u>design</u>, as mistakes made at this stage may be hard to correct   *Q40* later on.

The programme demonstrates that sustainable development is possible in areas where ...

PART 1

SALLY:	Good morning. Thanks for coming in to see us here at the agency, Joe. I'm one of the agency representatives, and my name's Sally Baker.
JOE:	Hi Sally. I think we spoke on the phone, didn't we?
SALLY:	That's right, we did. So thank you for sending in your CV. We've had quite a careful look at it and I think we have two jobs that might be suitable for you.
JOE:	OK.
SALLY:	The first one is in a company based in North London. They're looking for an administrative assistant.
JOE:	OK. What sort of company is it?
SALLY:	They're called Home Solutions and they design and make <u>furniture</u>.
JOE:	Oh, I don't know much about that, but it sounds interesting.
SALLY:	Yes, well as I said, they want someone in their office, and looking at your past experience it does look as if you fit quite a few of the requirements. So on your CV it appears you've done some data entry?
JOE:	Yes.
SALLY:	So that's one skill they want. Then they expect the person they appoint to attend <u>meetings</u> and take notes there …
JOE:	OK. I've done that before, yes.
SALLY:	And you'd need to be able to cope with general admin.
JOE:	Filing, and keeping records and so on? That should be OK. And in my last job I also had to manage the <u>diary</u>.
SALLY:	Excellent. That's something they want here too. I'd suggest you add it to your CV – I don't think you mentioned that, did you?
JOE:	No.
SALLY:	So as far as the requirements go, they want good computer skills, of course, and they particularly mention spreadsheets.
JOE:	That should be fine.
SALLY:	And interpersonal skills – which would be something they'd check with your references.
JOE:	I think that should be OK, yes.
SALLY:	Then they mention that they want someone who is careful and takes care with <u>details</u> – just looking at your CV, I'd say you're probably alright there.
JOE:	I think so, yes. Do they want any special experience?
SALLY:	I think they wanted some experience of teleconferencing.
JOE:	I've got three years' experience of that.
SALLY:	Let's see, yes, good. In fact they're only asking for <u>at least one year</u>, so that's great. So is that something that might interest you?
JOE:	It is, yes. The only thing is, you said they were in North London so it would be quite a long commute for me.
SALLY:	OK.

SALLY:	So the second position might suit you better as far as the location goes; that's for a warehouse assistant and that's in South London.
JOE:	Yes, that would be a lot closer.
SALLY:	And you've worked in a warehouse before, haven't you?
JOE:	Yes.

Q1

Q2

Q3

Q4

Q5

SALLY:	So as far as the responsibilities for this position go, they want someone who can manage the stock, obviously, and also <u>deliveries</u>.	Q6
JOE:	That should be OK. You've got to keep track of stuff, but I've always been quite good with numbers.	
SALLY:	Good. that's their first requirement. And they want someone who's computer literate, which we know you are.	
JOE:	Sure.	
SALLY:	Then they mention organisational skills. They want someone who's well organised.	
JOE:	Yes, I think I am.	
SALLY:	And <u>tidy</u>?	Q7
JOE:	Yes, they go together really, don't they?	
SALLY:	Sure. Then the usual stuff; they want someone who can communicate well both orally and in writing.	
JOE:	OK. And for the last warehouse job I had, one of the things I enjoyed most was being part of a <u>team</u>. I found that was really essential for the job.	Q8
SALLY:	Excellent. Yes, they do mention that they want someone who's used to that, yes. Now when you were working in a warehouse last time, what sorts of items were you dealing with?	
JOE:	It was mostly bathroom and kitchen equipment, sinks and stoves and fridges.	
SALLY:	So you're OK moving <u>heavy</u> things?	Q9
JOE:	Sure. I'm quite strong, and I've had the training.	
SALLY:	Good. Now as far as experience goes, they mention they want someone with a licence, and that you have experience of driving in London – so you can cope with the traffic and so on.	
JOE:	Yes, no problem.	
SALLY:	And you've got experience of warehouse work … and the final thing they mention is <u>customer</u> service. I think looking at your CV you're OK there.	Q10
JOE:	Right. So what about pay? Can you tell me a bit more about that, please …	

PART 2

PRESENTER:	My guest on the show today is Alice Riches who started the Street Play Scheme where she lives in Beechwood Road. For those of you that don't already know – Street Play involves local residents closing off their street for a few hours so that children have a chance to play in the street safely. She started it in her own street, Beechwood Road, and the idea caught on, and there are now Street Play Schemes all over the city. So when did you actually start the scheme, Alice?	
ALICE:	Well, I first had the idea when my oldest child was still a toddler, so that's about six years ago now – but it took at least two years of campaigning before we were actually able to make it happen. <u>So the scheme's been up and running for three years now</u>. We'd love to be able to close our road for longer – for the whole weekend, from Saturday morning until Sunday evening, for example. <u>At the moment it's just once a week</u>. But when we started it was only once a month. But we're working on it.	Q11 Q12
PRESENTER:	So what actually happens when Beechwood Road is closed?	
ALICE:	We have <u>volunteer wardens, mostly parents but some elderly residents too, who block off our road at either end</u>. The council have provided special signs but there's always a volunteer there to explain what's happening to any motorists. Generally, they're fine about it – we've only had to get the police involved once or twice.	Q13

Now I should explain that the road isn't completely closed to cars. But only residents' cars are allowed. If people really need to get in or out of Beechwood Road, it's not a problem – as long as they drive at under 20 kilometres per hour. But most people just decide not to use their cars during this time, or they park in another street. The wardens are only there to stop through traffic. | Q14

PRESENTER: So can anyone apply to get involved in Street Play?

ALICE: Absolutely – we want to include all kids in the city – especially those who live on busy roads. It's here that demand is greatest. Obviously, there isn't such demand in wealthier areas where the children have access to parks or large gardens – or in the suburbs where there are usually more places for children to play outside. | Q15

I'd recommend that anyone listening who likes the idea should just give it a go. We've been surprised by the positive reaction of residents all over the city. And that's not just parents. There are always a few who complain but they're a tiny minority. On the whole everyone is very supportive and say they're very happy to see children out on the street – even if it does get quite noisy. | Q16

ALICE: There have been so many benefits of Street Play for the kids. Parents really like the fact that the kids are getting fresh air instead of sitting staring at a computer screen, even if they're not doing anything particularly energetic. And of course it's great that kids can play with their friends outside without being supervised by their parents – but for me the biggest advantage is that kids develop confidence in themselves to be outside without their parents. The other really fantastic thing is that children get to know the adults in the street – it's like having a big extended family. | Q17/Q18 Q17/Q18

PRESENTER: It certainly does have a lot of benefits. I want to move on now and ask you about a related project in King Street.

ALICE: Right. Well this was an experiment I was involved in where local residents decided to try and reduce the traffic along King Street, which is the busiest main road in our area, by persuading people not to use their cars for one day. We thought about making people pay more for parking – but we decided that would be really unpopular – so instead we just stopped people from parking on King Street but left the other car parks open.

It was surprising how much of a difference all this made. As we'd predicted, air quality was significantly better but what I hadn't expected was how much quieter it would be – even with the buses still running. Of course everyone said they felt safer but we were actually amazed that sales in the shops went up considerably that day – we thought there'd be fewer people out shopping – not more. | Q19/Q20 Q19/Q20

PRESENTER: That's really interesting so the fact that …

PART 3

HAZEL: Tom, could I ask you for some advice, please?

TOM: Yes of course, if you think I can help. What's it about?

HAZEL: It's my first media studies assignment, and I'm not sure how to go about it. You must have done it last year.

TOM: Is that the one comparing the coverage of a particular story in a range of newspapers?

HAZEL: That's right.

TOM: Oh yes, I really enjoyed writing it.

HAZEL: So what sort of things do I need to compare?

TOM: Well, there are several things. For example, there's the question of which page of the newspaper the item appears on. | Q21

HAZEL:	You mean, because there's a big difference between having it on the front page and the bottom of page ten, for instance?	
TOM:	Exactly. And that shows how important the editor thinks the story is. Then there's the <u>size</u> – how many column inches the story is given, how many columns it spreads over.	Q22
HAZEL:	And I suppose that includes the headline.	
TOM:	It certainly does. It's all part of attracting the reader's attention.	
HAZEL:	What about <u>graphics</u> – whether there's anything visual in addition to the text?	Q23
TOM:	Yes, you need to consider those, too, because they can have a big effect on the reader's understanding of the story – sometimes a bigger effect than the text itself. Then you'll need to look at how the item is put together: what <u>structure</u> is it given? Bear in mind that not many people read beyond the first paragraph, so what has the journalist put at the beginning? And if, say, there are conflicting opinions about something, does one appear near the end, where people probably won't read it?	Q24
HAZEL:	And newspapers sometimes give wrong or misleading information, don't they? Either deliberately or by accident. Should I be looking at that, too?	
TOM:	Yes, if you can. Compare what's in different versions, and as far as possible, try and work out what's true and what isn't. And that relates to a very important point: what's the writer's <u>purpose</u>, or at least the most important one, if they have several. It may seem to be to inform the public, but often it's that they want to create fear, or controversy, or to make somebody look ridiculous.	Q25
HAZEL:	Gosh, I see what you mean. And I suppose the writer may make <u>assumptions</u> about the reader.	Q26
TOM:	That's right – about their knowledge of the subject, their attitudes, and their level of education, which means writing so that the readers understand without feeling patronised. All of that will make a difference to how the story is presented.	

HAZEL:	Does it matter what type of story I write about?	
TOM:	No – national or international politics, the arts ... Anything, as long as it's covered in two or three newspapers. Though of course it'll be easier and more fun if it's something you're interested in and know something about.	
HAZEL:	And on that basis <u>a national news item would be worth analysing – I'm quite keen on politics, so I'll try and find a suitable topic</u>. What did you choose for your analysis, Tom?	Q27
TOM:	I was interested in how newspapers express their opinions explicitly, so <u>I wanted to compare editorials in different papers, but when I started looking, I couldn't find two on the same topic</u> that I felt like analysing.	Q28
HAZEL:	In that case, <u>I won't even bother to look</u>.	
TOM:	So in the end I chose a human interest story – a terribly emotional story about a young girl who was very ill, and lots of other people – mostly strangers – raised money so she could go abroad for treatment. Actually, I was surprised – some papers just wrote about how wonderful everyone was, but others considered the broader picture, like why treatment wasn't available here.	
HAZEL:	Hmm, <u>I usually find stories like that raise quite strong feelings in me! I'll avoid that. Perhaps I'll choose an arts topic</u>, like different reviews of a film, or something about funding for the arts – I'll think about that.	Q29 Q30
TOM:	Yes, that might be interesting.	
HAZEL:	OK, well thanks a lot for your help, Tom. It's been really useful.	
TOM:	You're welcome. Good luck with the assignment, Hazel.	

PART 4

Nowadays, we use *different* products for personal cleanliness, laundry, dishwashing and household cleaning, but this is very much a 20th-century development.

The origins of cleanliness date back to prehistoric times. Since water is essential for life, the earliest people lived near water and knew something about its cleansing properties – at least that it rinsed mud off their hands.

Q31

During the excavation of ancient Babylon, evidence was found that soapmaking was known as early as 2800 BC. Archaeologists discovered cylinders made of clay, with inscriptions on them saying that fats were boiled with ashes. This is a method of making soap, though there's no reference to the purpose of this material.

Q32

The early Greeks bathed for aesthetic reasons and apparently didn't use soap. Instead, they cleaned their bodies with blocks of sand, pumice and ashes, then anointed themselves with oil, and scraped off the oil and dirt with a metal instrument known as a strigil. They also used oil mixed with ashes. Clothes were washed without soap in streams.

Q33

The ancient Germans and Gauls are also credited with discovering how to make a substance called 'soap', made of melted animal fat and ashes. They used this mixture to tint their hair red.

Q34

Soap got its name, according to an ancient Roman legend, from Mount Sapo, where animals were sacrificed, leaving deposits of animal fat. Rain washed these deposits, along with wood ashes, down into the clay soil along the River Tiber. Women found that this mixture greatly reduced the effort required to wash their clothes.

As Roman civilisation advanced, so did bathing. The first of the famous Roman baths, supplied with water from their aqueducts, was built about 312 BC. The baths were luxurious, and bathing became very popular. And by the second century AD, the Greek physician Galen recommended soap for both medicinal and cleansing purposes.

Q35

After the fall of Rome in 467 AD and the resulting decline in bathing habits, much of Europe felt the impact of filth on public health. This lack of personal cleanliness and related unsanitary living conditions were major factors in the outbreaks of disease in the Middle Ages, and especially the Black Death of the 14th century.

Q36

Nevertheless, soapmaking became an established craft in Europe, and associations of soapmakers guarded their trade secrets closely. Vegetable and animal oils were used with ashes of plants, along with perfume, apparently for the first time. Gradually more varieties of soap became available for shaving and shampooing, as well as bathing and laundering.

Q37

A major step toward large-scale commercial soapmaking occurred in 1791, when a French chemist, Nicholas Leblanc, patented a process for turning salt into soda ash, or sodium carbonate. Soda ash is the alkali obtained from ashes that combines with fat to form soap. The Leblanc process yielded quantities of good-quality, inexpensive soda ash.

Q38

Modern soapmaking was born some 20 years later, in the early 19th century, with the discovery by Michel Eugène Chevreul, another French chemist, of the chemical nature and relationship of fats, glycerine and fatty acids. His studies established the basis for both fat and soap chemistry, and soapmaking became a science. Further developments during the 19th century made it easier and cheaper to manufacture soap.

Q39

Until the 19th century, soap was regarded as a luxury item, and was heavily taxed in several countries. As it became more readily available, it became an everyday necessity, a development that was reinforced <u>when the high tax was removed</u>. Soap was then something ordinary people could afford, and cleanliness standards improved. **Q40**

With this widespread use came the development of milder soaps for bathing and soaps for use in the washing machines that were available to consumers by the turn of the 20th century.

TEST 4

PART 1

MAN:	Hello. Do you mind if I ask you some questions about your journey today? We're doing a customer satisfaction survey.
SOPHIE:	Yes. OK. I've got about ten minutes before my train home leaves. I'm on a day trip.
MAN:	Great. Thank you. So first of all, could you tell me your name?
SOPHIE:	It's Sophie Bird.
MAN:	Thank you. And would you mind telling me what you do?
SOPHIE:	I'm a <u>journalist</u>.

Q1

MAN:	Oh really? That must be interesting.
SOPHIE:	Yes. It is.
MAN:	So was the reason for your visit here today work?
SOPHIE:	Actually, it's my day off. I came here to do some <u>shopping</u>.

Q2

MAN:	Oh right.
SOPHIE:	But I do sometimes come here for work.
MAN:	OK. Now I'd like to ask some questions about your journey today, if that's OK.
SOPHIE:	Yes. No problem.
MAN:	Right, so can you tell me which station you're travelling back to?
SOPHIE:	<u>Staunfirth</u>, where I live.

Q3

MAN:	Can I just check the spelling? S-T-A-U-N-F-I-R-T-H?
SOPHIE:	That's right.
MAN:	And you travelled from there this morning?
SOPHIE:	Yes.
MAN:	OK, good. Next, can I ask what kind of ticket you bought? I assume it wasn't a season ticket, as you don't travel every day.
SOPHIE:	That's right. No, I just got a normal <u>return</u> ticket. I don't have a rail card so I didn't get any discount. I keep meaning to get one because it's a lot cheaper.

Q4

MAN:	Yes – you'd have saved 20% on your ticket today. So you paid the full price for your ticket?
SOPHIE:	I paid <u>£23.70</u>.

Q5

MAN:	OK. Do you think that's good value for money?
SOPHIE:	Not really. I think it's too much for a journey that only takes 45 minutes.
MAN:	Yes, that's one of the main complaints we get. So, you didn't buy your ticket in advance?
SOPHIE:	No. I know it's cheaper if you buy a week in advance but I didn't know I was coming then.
MAN:	I know. You can't always plan ahead. So, did you buy it this morning?
SOPHIE:	No, it was yesterday.
MAN:	Right. And do you usually buy your tickets at the station?
SOPHIE:	Well, I do usually but the ticket office closes early and I hate using ticket machines. I think ticket offices should be open for longer hours. There's always a queue for the machines and they're often out of order.
MAN:	A lot of customers are saying the same thing.
SOPHIE:	So to answer your question… I got an e-ticket <u>online</u>.

Q6

MAN:	OK. Thank you. Now I'd like to ask you about your satisfaction with your journey. So what would you say you were most satisfied with today?

SOPHIE:	Well, I like the wifi on the train. It's improved a lot. It makes it easier for me to work if I want to.
MAN:	That's the first time today anyone's mentioned that. It's good to get some positive feedback on that.
SOPHIE:	Mmm.
MAN:	And, is there anything you weren't satisfied with?
SOPHIE:	Well, normally, the trains run on time and are pretty reliable but today there was a delay; the train was about 15 minutes behind schedule.
MAN:	OK. I'll put that down. Now I'd also like to ask about the facilities at this station. You've probably noticed that the whole station's been upgraded. What are you most satisfied with?
SOPHIE:	I think the best thing is that they've improved the amount of information about train times etc. that's given to passengers – it's much clearer – before there was only one board and I couldn't always see it properly – which was frustrating.
MAN:	That's good. And is there anything you're not satisfied with?
SOPHIE:	Let's see … I think things have generally improved a lot. The trains are much more modern and I like the new café. But one thing is that there aren't enough places to sit down, especially on the platforms.
MAN:	OK – so I'll put 'seating' down, shall I, as the thing you're least satisfied with?
SOPHIE:	Yes. OK.
MAN:	Can I ask your opinion about some of the other facilities? We'd like feedback on whether people are satisfied, dissatisfied or neither satisfied nor dissatisfied.
SOPHIE:	OK.
MAN:	What about the parking at the station?
SOPHIE:	Well to be honest, I don't really have an opinion as I never use it.
MAN:	So, neither satisfied nor dissatisfied for that then.
SOPHIE:	Yes, I suppose so …
MAN:	OK, and what about …?

Q7 appears beside the "delay" line.
Q8 appears beside the "information" line.
Q9 appears beside the "platforms" line.
Q10 appears beside the "parking" line.

PART 2

As chair of the town council subcommittee on park facilities, I'd like to bring you up to date on some of the changes that have been made recently to the Croft Valley Park. So if you could just take a look at the map I handed out, let's begin with a general overview. So the basic arrangement of the park hasn't changed – it still has two gates, north and south, and a lake in the middle.

The café continues to serve an assortment of drinks and snacks and is still in the same place, looking out over the lake and next to the old museum.   Q11

We're hoping to change the location of the toilets, and bring them nearer to the centre of the park as they're a bit out of the way at present, near the adventure playground, in the corner of   Q12
your map.

The formal gardens have been replanted and should be at their best in a month or two. They used to be behind the old museum, but we've now used the space near the south gate –   Q13
between the park boundary and the path that goes past the lake towards the old museum.

We have a new outdoor gym for adults and children, which is already proving very popular. It's by the glass houses, just to the right of the path from the south gate. You have to look for   Q14
it as it's a bit hidden in the trees.

One very successful introduction has been our skateboard ramp. It's in constant use during the evenings and holidays. It's <u>near the old museum, at the end of a little path that leads off</u> <u>from the main path between the lake and the museum.</u>　　Q15

We've also introduced a new area for wild flowers, to attract bees and butterflies. It's <u>on</u> 　　Q16
<u>a bend in the path that goes round the east side of the lake, just south of the adventure</u> <u>playground.</u>

Now let me tell you a bit more about some of the changes to Croft Valley Park.

One of our most exciting developments has been the adventure playground. We were aware that we had nowhere for children to let off steam, and decided to use our available funds to set up a completely new facility in a large space to the north of the park. It's open year-round, though it closes early in the winter months, and <u>entrance is completely free</u>. Children can 　　Q17/Q18
choose whatever activities they want to do, irrespective of their age, but <u>we do ask adults not</u> 　　Q17/Q18
<u>to leave them on their own there.</u> There are plenty of seats where parents can relax and keep an eye on their children at the same time.

Lastly, the glass houses. A huge amount of work has been done on them to repair the <u>damage following the disastrous fire that recently destroyed their western side.</u> Over £80,000 　　Q19/Q20
was spent on replacing the glass walls and the metal supports, as well as the plants that had been destroyed, although unfortunately the collection of tropical palm trees has proved too expensive to replace up to now. At present the glass houses are open from 10am to 3pm <u>Mondays to Thursdays, and it's hoped to extend this to the weekend soon.</u> We're grateful to 　　Q19/Q20
all those who helped us by contributing their time and money to this achievement.

The gardens have …

PART 3

ANNIE:	OK, Jack. Before we plan our presentation about refrigeration, let's discuss what we've discovered so far.
JACK:	Fine, Annie. Though I have to admit I haven't done much research yet.
ANNIE:	Nor me. But I found an interesting article about icehouses. I'd seen some 18th- and 19th-century ones here in the UK, so I knew they were often built in a shady area or underground, close to lakes that might freeze in the winter. Then blocks of ice could be cut and stored in the icehouse. But <u>I didn't realise that insulating</u> <u>the blocks with straw or sawdust meant they didn't melt for months.</u> The ancient Romans had refrigeration, too.
JACK:	I didn't know that.
ANNIE:	Yes, pits were dug in the ground, and snow was imported from the mountains – even though they were at quite a distance. The snow was stored in the pits. Ice formed at the bottom of it. <u>Both the ice and the snow were then sold.</u> The ice cost more than the snow and my guess is that only the wealthy members of society could afford it.
JACK:	I wouldn't be surprised. I also came across an article about modern domestic fridges. Several different technologies are used, but they were too complex for me to understand.
ANNIE:	You have to wonder what happens when people get rid of old ones.
JACK:	You mean because the gases in them are harmful for the environment?

Q21 (aligned with "I didn't realise that insulating")

Q22 (aligned with "Both the ice and the snow were then sold.")

ANNIE:	Exactly. At least there are now plenty of organisations that will recycle most of the components safely, but of course <u>some people just dump old fridges in the countryside</u>.	Q23
JACK:	<u>It's hard to see how they can be stopped unfortunately</u>. In the UK we get rid of three million a year altogether!	
ANNIE:	That sounds a lot, especially because fridges hardly ever break down.	
JACK:	That's right. In this country we keep domestic fridges for 11 years on average, and a lot last for 20 or more. So <u>if you divide the cost by the number of years you can use a fridge, they're not expensive, compared with some household appliances</u>.	Q24
ANNIE:	<u>True</u>. I suppose manufacturers encourage people to spend more by making them different colours and designs. I'm sure when my parents bought their first fridge they had hardly any choice!	
JACK:	Yes, there's been quite a change.	

JACK:	Right, let's make a list of topics to cover in our presentation, and decide who's going to do more research on them. Then later, we can get together and plan the next step.	
ANNIE:	OK. How about starting with how useful refrigeration is, and <u>the range of goods that are refrigerated</u> nowadays? Because of course it's not just food and drinks.	Q25
JACK:	No, I suppose flowers and medicines are refrigerated, too.	
ANNIE:	And computers. <u>I could do that</u>, unless you particularly want to.	
JACK:	No, that's fine by me. What about <u>the effects of refrigeration on people's health</u>? After all, some of the chemicals used in the 19th century were pretty harmful, but there have been lots of benefits too, like always having access to fresh food. Do you fancy dealing with that?	Q26
ANNIE:	I'm not terribly keen, to be honest.	
JACK:	Nor me. My mind just goes blank when I read anything about chemicals.	
ANNIE:	<u>Oh, all right then, I'll do you a favour</u>. But you owe me, Jack. OK. What about <u>the effects on food producers</u>, like farmers in poorer countries being able to export their produce to developed countries? Something for you, maybe?	Q27
JACK:	<u>I don't mind</u>. It should be quite interesting.	
ANNIE:	I think we should also look at <u>how refrigeration has helped whole cities</u> – like Las Vegas, which couldn't exist without refrigeration because it's in the middle of a desert.	Q28
JACK:	Right. I had a quick look at an economics book in the library that's got a chapter about this sort of thing. I could give you the title, if you want to do this section.	
ANNIE:	Not particularly, to be honest. I find economics books pretty heavy going, as a rule.	
JACK:	<u>OK, leave it to me, then</u>.	
ANNIE:	Thanks. Then there's transport, and the difference that <u>refrigerated trucks</u> have made. <u>I wouldn't mind having a go at that</u>.	Q29
JACK:	Don't forget trains, too. I read something about milk and butter being transported in refrigerated railroad cars in the USA, right back in the 1840s.	
ANNIE:	I hadn't thought of trains. Thanks.	
JACK:	Shall we have a separate section on <u>domestic fridges</u>? After all, they're something everyone's familiar with.	Q30

ANNIE: <u>What about splitting it into two</u>? You could investigate 19th- and 20th-century fridges, and I'll concentrate on what's available these days, and how manufacturers differentiate their products from those of their competitors.

JACK: <u>OK, that'd suit me.</u>

PART 4

Hi everyone, in this session I'll be presenting my research about the social history of Britain during the Industrial Revolution. I particularly looked at how ordinary lives were affected by changes that happened at that time. This was a time that saw the beginning of a new phenomenon: consumerism – where buying and selling goods became a major part of ordinary people's lives.

In fact, it was in the 19th century that the quantity and quality of people's possessions was used as an indication of the <u>wealth</u> of the country. Before this, the vast majority of people had very few possessions, but all that was changed by the Industrial Revolution. This was the era from the mid-18th to the late 19th century, when improvements in how goods were made as well as in <u>technology</u> triggered massive social changes that transformed life for just about everybody in several key areas.

Q31

Q32

First let's look at manufacturing. When it comes to manufacturing, we tend to think of the Industrial Revolution in images of steam engines and coal. And it's true that the Industrial Revolution couldn't have taken place at all if it weren't for these new sources of <u>power</u>. They marked an important shift away from the traditional watermills and windmills that had dominated before this. The most advanced industry for much of the 19th century was <u>textiles</u>. This meant that fashionable fabrics, and lace and ribbons were made available to everyone.

Q33

Q34

Before the Industrial Revolution, most people made goods to sell in small workshops, often in their own homes. But enormous new <u>machines</u> were now being created that could produce the goods faster and on a larger scale, and these required a lot more space. So large factories were built, replacing the workshops, and forcing workers to travel to work. In fact, large numbers of people migrated from villages into towns as a result.

Q35

As well as manufacturing, there were new technologies in transport, contributing to the growth of consumerism. The horse-drawn stagecoaches and carts of the 18th century, which carried very few people and goods, and travelled slowly along poorly surfaced roads, were gradually replaced by the numerous canals that were constructed. These were particularly important for the transportation of goods. The canals gradually fell out of use, though, as railways were developed, becoming the main way of moving goods and people from one end of the country to the other. And the goods they moved weren't just coal, iron, clothes, and so on – significantly, they included <u>newspapers</u>, which meant that thousands of people were not only more knowledgeable about what was going on in the country, but could also read about what was available in the shops. And that encouraged them to buy more. So faster forms of transport resulted in distribution becoming far more efficient – goods could now be sold all over the country, instead of just in the <u>local</u> market.

Q36

Q37

The third main area that saw changes that contributed to consumerism was retailing. The number and quality of shops grew rapidly, and in particular, small shops suffered as customers flocked to the growing number of department stores – a form of retailing that was new in the 19th century. The entrepreneurs who opened these found new ways to stock them with goods, and to attract customers: for instance, improved <u>lighting</u> inside *Q38* greatly increased the visibility of the goods for sale. Another development that made goods more visible from outside resulted from the use of plate glass, which made it possible for <u>windows</u> to be much larger than previously. New ways of promoting goods *Q39* were introduced, too. Previously, the focus had been on *informing* potential customers about the availability of goods; now there was an explosion in <u>advertising</u> trying to *Q40* persuade people to go shopping.

Flanders claims that one of the great effects of the Industrial Revolution was that it created choice. All sorts of things that had previously been luxuries – from sugar to cutlery – became conveniences, and before long they'd turned into necessities: life without sugar or cutlery was unimaginable. Rather like mobile phones these days!

Listening and Reading answer keys

LISTENING

 Answer key with extra explanations in Resource bank

Part 1, Questions 1–10

1 Jamieson
2 afternoon
3 communication
4 week
5 10/ten
6 suit
7 passport
8 personality
9 feedback
10 time

Part 2, Questions 11–20

11 A
12 B
13 A
14 C
15 river
16 1422
17 top
18 pass
19 steam
20 capital

Part 3, Questions 21–30

21 G
22 F
23 A
24 E
25 B
26 C
27 C
28 A
29&30 *IN EITHER ORDER*
　　　B
　　　D

Part 4, Questions 31–40

31 shelter
32 oil
33 roads
34 insects
35 grass(es)
36 water
37 soil
38 dry
39 simple
40 nest(s)

If you score …

0–17	18–27	28–40
you are unlikely to get an acceptable score under examination conditions and we recommend that you spend a lot of time improving your English before you take IELTS.	you may get an acceptable score under examination conditions but we recommend that you think about having more practice or lessons before you take IELTS.	you are likely to get an acceptable score under examination conditions but remember that different institutions will find different scores acceptable.

TEST 1

READING

 Answer key with extra explanations in Resource bank

Reading Section 1, Questions 1–14

1	NOT GIVEN
2	NOT GIVEN
3	TRUE
4	TRUE
5	FALSE
6	NOT GIVEN
7	D
8	E
9	B
10	A
11	D
12	B
13	E
14	C

Reading Section 2, Questions 15–27

15	3 / three metres / meters
16	residential building sites
17	eliminate
18	(temporary) (work) platforms
19	safety nets
20	(maintenance) work

21	selection
22	inspection
23	140.98
24	unemployed
25	payslip
26	doctor's letter
27	circumstances

Reading Section 3, Questions 28–40

28	D
29	C
30	C
31	D
32	C
33	F
34	B
35	A
36	G
37	gravel
38	nuggets
39	sieve
40	mercury

If you score ...

0–24	25–31	32–40
you are unlikely to get an acceptable score under examination conditions and we recommend that you spend a lot of time improving your English before you take IELTS.	you may get an acceptable score under examination conditions but we recommend that you think about having more practice or lessons before you take IELTS.	you are likely to get an acceptable score under examination conditions but remember that different institutions will find different scores acceptable.

TEST 2

LISTENING

 Answer key with extra explanations in Resource bank

Part 1, Questions 1–10

1 Eustatis
2 review
3 dance
4 *Chat*
5 healthy
6 posters
7 wood
8 lake
9 insects
10 blog

Part 2, Questions 11–20

11 C
12 A
13 B
14 C
15 E
16 C
17 B
18 A
19 G
20 D

Part 3, Questions 21–30

21&22 *IN EITHER ORDER*
      B
      D
23&24 *IN EITHER ORDER*
      B
      C
25 G
26 B
27 D
28 C
29 H
30 F

Part 4, Questions 31–40

31 irrigation
32 women
33 wire(s)
34 seed(s)
35 posts
36 transport
37 preservation
38 fish(es)
39 bees
40 design

If you score …

0–18	19–27	28–40
you are unlikely to get an acceptable score under examination conditions and we recommend that you spend a lot of time improving your English before you take IELTS.	you may get an acceptable score under examination conditions but we recommend that you think about having more practice or lessons before you take IELTS.	you are likely to get an acceptable score under examination conditions but remember that different institutions will find different scores acceptable.

TEST 2

READING

 Answer key with extra explanations in Resource bank

Reading Section 1,
Questions 1–14

1	FALSE
2	NOT GIVEN
3	TRUE
4	TRUE
5	FALSE
6	FALSE
7	C
8	A
9	C
10	B
11	C
12	E
13	B
14	D

Reading Section 2,
Questions 15–27

15	sewage
16	poisoning
17	drowning
18	gloves
19	tags
20	disconnected
21	objectives
22	review
23	calendar
24	collaboration
25	distraction
26	creativity
27	retention

Reading Section 3,
Questions 28–40

28	iv
29	vi
30	vii
31	i
32	v
33	iii
34	A
35	C
36	D
37	B
38	flexible
39	land
40	ball

If you score ...

0–25	26–32	33–40
you are unlikely to get an acceptable score under examination conditions and we recommend that you spend a lot of time improving your English before you take IELTS.	you may get an acceptable score under examination conditions but we recommend that you think about having more practice or lessons before you take IELTS.	you are likely to get an acceptable score under examination conditions but remember that different institutions will find different scores acceptable.

TEST 3

LISTENING

 Answer key with extra explanations
in Resource bank

Part 1, Questions 1–10

1 furniture
2 meetings
3 diary
4 detail(s)
5 1 / one year
6 deliveries
7 tidy
8 team
9 heavy
10 customer

Part 2, Questions 11–20

11 B
12 A
13 C
14 B
15 C
16 B
17&18 *IN EITHER ORDER*
  B
  D
19&20 *IN EITHER ORDER*
  A
  E

Part 3, Questions 21–30

21 page
22 size
23 graphic(s)
24 structure
25 purpose
26 assumption(s)
27 A
28 C
29 C
30 B

Part 4, Questions 31–40

31 mud
32 clay
33 metal
34 hair
35 bath(s)
36 disease(s)
37 perfume
38 salt
39 science
40 tax

If you score …

0–17	18–27	28–40
you are unlikely to get an acceptable score under examination conditions and we recommend that you spend a lot of time improving your English before you take IELTS.	you may get an acceptable score under examination conditions but we recommend that you think about having more practice or lessons before you take IELTS.	you are likely to get an acceptable score under examination conditions but remember that different institutions will find different scores acceptable.

TEST 3

READING

 Answer key with extra explanations in Resource bank

Reading Section 1, Questions 1–14

1 FALSE
2 TRUE
3 NOT GIVEN
4 TRUE
5 FALSE
6 NOT GIVEN
7 TRUE
8 B
9 E
10 C
11 D
12 A
13 F
14 C

Reading Section 2, Questions 15–27

15 familiar
16 abilities
17 stimulating
18 potential
19 promotion
20 flexible

21 C
22 F
23 C
24 A
25 E
26 B
27 D

Reading Section 3, Questions 28–40

28 D
29 A
30 B
31 efficient
32 food
33 hibernation
34 blood
35 temperature
36 A
37 D
38 B
39 C
40 A

If you score ...

0–24	25–31	32–40
you are unlikely to get an acceptable score under examination conditions and we recommend that you spend a lot of time improving your English before you take IELTS.	you may get an acceptable score under examination conditions but we recommend that you think about having more practice or lessons before you take IELTS.	you are likely to get an acceptable score under examination conditions but remember that different institutions will find different scores acceptable.

TEST 4

LISTENING

 Answer key with extra explanations in Resource bank

Part 1, Questions 1–10

1 journalist
2 shopping
3 Staunfirth
4 return
5 23.70
6 online
7 delay
8 information
9 platform(s)
10 parking

Part 2, Questions 11–20

11 D
12 C
13 G
14 H
15 A
16 E
17&18 *IN EITHER ORDER*
   A
   D
19&20 *IN EITHER ORDER*
   A
   C

Part 3, Questions 21–30

21 B
22 A
23 B
24 A
25 A
26 A
27 B
28 B
29 A
30 C

Part 4, Questions 31–40

31 wealth
32 technology
33 power
34 textile(s)
35 machines
36 newspapers
37 local
38 lighting
39 windows
40 Advertising

If you score …

0–18	19–27	28–40
you are unlikely to get an acceptable score under examination conditions and we recommend that you spend a lot of time improving your English before you take IELTS.	you may get an acceptable score under examination conditions but we recommend that you think about having more practice or lessons before you take IELTS.	you are likely to get an acceptable score under examination conditions but remember that different institutions will find different scores acceptable.

TEST 4

READING

 Answer key with extra explanations in Resource bank

Reading Section 1, Questions 1–14

1   E
2   C
3   B
4   D
5   A
6   C
7   B
8   NOT GIVEN
9   TRUE
10 TRUE
11 TRUE
12 FALSE
13 NOT GIVEN
14 FALSE

Reading Section 2, Questions 15–27

15 photo
16 screens
17 productivity
18 mobile
19 gossip
20 snacks

21 skills
22 commitment
23 value
24 panel
25 potential
26 organisation / organization
27 courses

Reading Section 3, Questions 28–40

28 rules
29 fairness
30 submissive
31 biting
32 forgiveness
33 E
34 C
35 G
36 D
37 F
38 C
39 D
40 B

If you score ...

0–23	24–30	31–40
you are unlikely to get an acceptable score under examination conditions and we recommend that you spend a lot of time improving your English before you take IELTS.	you may get an acceptable score under examination conditions but we recommend that you think about having more practice or lessons before you take IELTS.	you are likely to get an acceptable score under examination conditions but remember that different institutions will find different scores acceptable.

Sample Writing answers

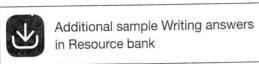 Additional sample Writing answers in Resource bank

TEST 1, WRITING TASK 1

This is an answer written by a candidate who achieved a **Band 6.0** score.

Dear Emily,

I haven't seen you for a long time so Iam very excited to meet you. I know that you are thinking of going on a camping holiday this summer for the first time. Iam very happy about that and Iam always ready to give you some advice.

Camping holiday is a wonderful idea. Especially in this summer. I think that not only do you want to go camping holiday in summer but also a lot of people because that is the best time for people to enjoy the life after hard-working day. One of the most important reason why you should go camping is that you are able to see the views and meet a lot of people. That is a chance for you to understand more a lot of culture in our country which you have never known before. The other reason is that you can take part in some social activities which are very interesting. On the other hand, going camping in the summer has a lot of disadvantages. In the first place, it will have negative impact on your skin so you have to wear hat before going camping outside. Secondly, it is easy for you to be ill because the weather in summer is quite hot so you have to prepare medicines before. I would also like to go camping with you this summer because my holiday in summer is very long so I hope that you can go on a camping holiday with me.

Hope to meet you soon.

Your close friend

Here is the examiner's comment:

The writer has addressed all three bullet points and organisation of the information is generally clear. There is some repetition [*camping holiday*] which could be avoided by using alternative words or phrases e.g. *this kind of holiday*. The range of vocabulary is sufficient for the task and there is some good use of collocation [*a wonderful idea | the best time | see the views | meet a lot of people | understand more a lot of culture | take part in some social activities*]. There is a mix of simple and complex structures with a fair level of accuracy. Occasional errors occur [*Iam / I am | Especially in this summer* (sentence fragment) | *One of the most important reason*(s) | *it will have* (a) *negative impact on | prepare medicines before /* in advance], but the meaning is still clear.

TEST 1, WRITING TASK 2

This is an answer written by a candidate who achieved a **Band 7.5** score.

The reason behind the rising popularity of the crime novels and TV dramas, lies with the fact that the reality transmitted in the show/book, is our own. I am from Rio de Janeiro, a beautiful place with horrible people, and we know that what soap operas show, is not our reality. Sometimes happy endings only happen in fairytales, which leads me to "Tropa de Elite" (Elite Squad, roughly translated) and why it was a phenomenon.

The movie shows our dark side, the drug dealers with machine guns, the dangerous environment of the favelas and the corruption in our police forces. It shows that there is nothing glamorous about being poor in Brazil (an idea that has been growing lately). And that? We relate. We know the truth, and we want it to be seen and heard, even if it is a fiction vision of it.

this is where the fiction part enters. When we watch the brave policeman or the brilliant CSI save the day, it gives a slight comfort. We feel like someone can save us from our reality, someone can be our hero and get the job done. It is a rather gullible thought, but it is the truth. BOPE's popularity (Rio de Janeiro's elite police force) grew rapidly after the movie's success.

want to feel heard and to be saved, and in a mix of reality and fantasy, these books and shows do that. I, for example, love them and even considered to be a police officer. But after careful consideration, i gave up the idea, for i think the world's salvation lies behind a pen or inside a book, and not on the tip of a machine gun. But there is nothing wrong to daydream on our favorite shows.

Here is the examiner's comment:

> This is a thoughtful response to the task and the writer explores both parts in some depth. The ideas are relevant, extended and well-supported. Information and ideas are logically organised and there is a clear progression throughout the answer. Paragraphing is handled well, with a clear central topic in each one. The range of vocabulary shows less common items [*transmitted | phenomenon | corruption | glamorous | salvation*] and good use of collocations [*rising popularity | soap operas | dark side | drug dealers | save the day*]. Errors in word formation are rare [*fiction / fictional vision*]. There is a variety of complex structures, well-controlled for accuracy, with only rare errors [*considered to be / being a police officer | nothing wrong to daydream / in daydreaming*]. Punctuation is generally well-controlled, apart from some lack of capitalisation in the final paragraph.

TEST 2, WRITING TASK 1

This is an answer written by a candidate who achieved a **Band 6.0** score.

Dear Sir or Madam,

I saw an advert that said that people that want to do voluntary at this museum should contact you. That's why I am writing this letter!

I would like to do voluntary work at your museum. I am keen on art and history, and especially I am keen on working with them. From what I kow, your museum is based on works of art that have fabulous history.

In the museum I could work as a guide. I already know some interesting information about the drawings that you have in the museum, but if there is something that I don't know or something that needs improvement, I am opened to studying and developing my knowledge.

I really like working with other people and explaining things that they are interested in, and that is a good skill I guess for guiding.

I am free every Monday, Friday and Sunday from 3PM to 7PM.

I am waiting for your reply and I hope that you agree with my voluntary work.

Here is the examiner's comment:

> The writer has made a fair attempt at the task, covering all three bullet points, with the second bullet point covered in more depth than the first and the third. Organisation is logical and there is a clear overall progression, slightly spoiled by the lack of a closing formula (Yours faithfully). The range of vocabulary is sufficient for the task [*advert* | *contact you* | *keen on* | *work as a guide* | *drawings* | *studying and developing my knowledge* | *working with other people*] and there are only minor errors [*kow* / know | *opened* / open]. There is a mix of simple and complex structures, generally used accurately, although there is a minor error in the lack of an article [*have (a) fabulous history*]. The score could be improved by expanding on the first and third bullet points and by using a wider range of grammatical structures.

TEST 2, WRITING TASK 2

This is an answer written by a candidate who achieved a **Band 7.0** score.

In the modern world, it is argued that sleeping is not taking seriously as before. Some factors which influence this trend can be managed. This essay will discuss problems caused by lack of sleep and give possible solutions to avoid lack of sleep. It will outline the ineffeciency of human beings as a result of lack of sleep and point at the importance to reducing work overload to sleep well as well as mantaining diet, physical and mental health.

Lack of sleep can cause inefficiency in human beings which results in accidents. Fatigue and tiredness tend to overwhelm human beings when they lack sleeping. The body requires enough rest and when this is not permitted it will shut down anytime. Overworking causes body to be sore. A body which is sore from overworking might not get enough from a sleep but requires treatment. Accidents in roads and at work are sometimes a result of non sleeping people. When a body is sore performance is decreased. It is advised to take enough sleep in order to perform duties swiftly. Accidents causes serious damage in human life there it is encouraged to take enough sleep to avoid mishaps.

It is now an individual call to be responsible in doing what is best to avoid consequencies of not sleeping. Reducing work overload is of the solution to combat fatigue. It is not advisable to work overload as this causes the body to be sore. Healthy eating according to dieticians provide remedies to human health. This greatly constitutes to the communications of mind and body and work for those who are consistent on the practice. Normal hours of working time per day and correct diet is essential in mainting a wonderful balance in sleep and work.

In conclusion sleeping is essential. Work overloads should be reduced and deiting as well as physical health are encouraged. Governments and stakeholders must pernalise those who work overwork themselves by more tax.

Here is the examiner's comment:

The writer addresses both parts of the task, presenting ideas and developing them. The writer's viewpoint is clear throughout the text. Ideas are organised logically, there is a clear progression and each paragraph has a clear central topic. The range of vocabulary shows a number of less common items [*fatigue* | *overwhelm* | *treatment* | *performance* | *mishaps* | *combat* | *dieticians* | *remedies*] although there are occasional errors in spelling [*ineffeciency* / inefficiency | *mantaining* / maintaining | *consequencies* / consequences | *mainting* / maintaining | *deiting* / dieting | *pernalise* / penalise] and word choice [*constitutes* / contributes]. The word [*sore*] is overused and there are occasional errors in the use of dependent prepositions e.g. [*point at* / out | *importance to* / of]. There is a variety of complex structures used with good grammatical control. Occasional errors occur [*is not taking* (taken as) *seriously* (as) | *causes* (the) *body* | *is* (one) *of the solution*(s)] but the majority of sentences are error-free.

TEST 3, WRITING TASK 1

This is an answer written by a candidate who achieved a **Band 7.0** score.

Dear William,

I hope this letter finds you well.

As per your request, regarding advice, I am writing you so that you can have some more information about the course, the university and the application process.

First of all, the course I studied was Intensive English, offered either in the morning or the evening. The one in the morning goes from 7 to 11am Monday to Thursday, on the other hand, the one in the evening is from 5 to 9pm on the same days. The whole course is 8 weeks. They are always taught by the best teachers, that's really motivating.

As a second point, the university. It's so organized! Besides, it's near where you live so access is easy. The cost is something you can pay monthly and they give you different options. The university really cares for your learning process so they also offer a tutor to help you if needed. I really recommend you the institution.

In order to fullfill the application, you just have to call the number of registration office and the receptionist will ask you for the course code, whic is 139, and some personal details. She'll let you know when the course starts.

I hope you find it useful! Do not hesitate to contact me again.

Regards, Jeanine

Here is the examiner's comment:

> This letter covers all three bullet points in some depth, as ideas are developed and extended for each bullet point. Information is logically organised and there is a clear progression throughout the script. Cohesive devices are used well [*First of all* | *Besides* | *In order to*] and there is use of reference [*They*] and substitution [*The one in the morning* | *the one in the evening* | *the same days*]. There are some examples of less common vocabulary [*motivating* | *access* | *learning process* | *institution* | *receptionist*] and there are only occasional spelling errors [*whic* / which]. There is a variety of complex structures showing a good level of grammatical control.

TEST 3, WRITING TASK 2

This is an answer written by a candidate who achieved a **Band 6.0** score.

Our world is fulled of amazing places and almost every people would to visit such ones. On holiday they are given this opportunity and people leave their country and travel. But what they will choose in the future?

In my opinion, most people will prefer to spend their holidays travelling. First of all, people are fed up with own country and they will be in the future, especially. They want to try and see something new. Secondly, travelling improves language skills, broadens the horizons, gives an opportunity to communicate with foreigns. People learn about culture, taste local food. Thirdly, they get an brilliant experience which they will never forget.

Nevertheless, it is believed that people will leave in own country. To begin with, there are a lot of places in their country which is worth to visit. People think that it is enough for them. There will be more entertainment and interesting places in the future than nowadays. Of course, people will not want to go far if they have everything what the need in own country. What is more, much money is spent on travelling, so people will save it and travel towns in their country only.

I do not agree with this opinion. I think, people will a lot of opportunities to earn money in the future as the world is developing very quickly. So they can afford travelling.

To sum up, travelling abroad on holiday has as many advantages as staying at own country. But I strongly believe that people should not afraid of leaving their country. I hope, they will search another places all over the world.

Here is the examiner's comment:

> The candidate looks at both points of view, presenting and developing ideas for each one as well as giving his/her own point of view early on in the answer. Organisation is evident and there is a clear overall progression. Some cohesive devices are used to guide the reader through the response [*In my opinion* | *First of all* | *Secondly* | *Thirdly* | *Nevertheless* | *To begin with* | *I think* | *So* | *To sum up*]. The range of vocabulary is sufficient for the task [*amazing places* | *travelling* | *see something new* | *broadens the horizons* | *entertainment*], although there are some errors in word formation and spelling [*fulled* / full *of* | *leave* / live | *foreigns* / foreigners | *another* / other *places*]. The meaning is still clear, however. There is a mix of simple and complex sentence structures, with a reasonable degree of accuracy. Sometimes words are omitted [*every people would* (like) *to visit* | *in* (their) *own country* | *travel* (to) *towns* | *will* (have) *a lot of opportunities* | *should not* (be) *afraid*] and there are some lapses in grammatical control [*But what they will* / But what will they | *which is* / are *worth to visit* / visiting | *everything what* / that *the* / they *need*], but again the meaning is still clear.

TEST 4, WRITING TASK 1

This is an answer written by a candidate who achieved a **Band 7.0** score.

Dear Sir and Madam,

I am a long standing Indian citizen who works as a professor in the Giujarat University, Guijarat, India. I am writing this to apply for a job at Hindi language teacher, what you are looking for your chids.

The foremost reason of applying for a job is I have done PHD in Hinda literature successfully from the reputed Giujarat Univerity of India. Besides this I am teaching the Hindi language professionally since last 15 years. I have a wide experience of teaching among different institutions and from the children to younger one. Considering all these factors I feel that I am a suitable candidate for this job.

Moreover, I can also teach the Hindi language to other family member if required so I can make you all aware about Indian culture and its traditions, as I have a vast knowledge of all that too.

As I already have so many years in my home country India, now I want to migrate to different nations of the world so I can learn about the people, their culture and traditions. I will also provide me the opportunity to gain knowledge and some invaluable experiences. I strongly feel that coming to Australia could be great opportunity for me.

In anticipation waiting for your positive response at earliest.

Yours faithfull,

Vipal

Here is the examiner's comment:

> This is a quite formal letter of application, but the tone is consistent throughout and all three bullet points are addressed, extended and supported. Information is logically organised and there is a clear progression throughout the answer. Cohesive devices are used and paragraphing is appropriate. The range of vocabulary is sufficient to show some less common items [*long standing* | *citizen* | *invaluable*] and collocations [*wide experience* | *suitable candidate* | *vast knowledge* | *great opportunity*], although there are occasional errors [*Giujarat* / Gujarat | *at* / as | *chids* / children or kids | *Hinda* / Hindu | *family member*(s) | *I will* / It will | *faithfull* / faithfully]. Similarly, the grammatical range is wide enough to demonstrate a variety of complex structures, used with a good level of accuracy. There are occasional errors in the use of articles and tenses, but the majority of sentences are error-free.

TEST 4, WRITING TASK 2

This is an answer written by a candidate who achieved a **Band 6.5** score.

Technology nowadays is playing a major role in day-to-day life. It has made almost all activities very much easier. It has given us many benefits. One of the major benefits in today's life is 'Online Payment'. Today, I am going to highlight the positives and negatives of the same.

When the E-commerce websites were launched, people were very much pleased with the option of paying online, but they consider bit risky then. Net-Banking was not that very common. People were not able to believe or put trust Therefore, they preferred 'Cash-On-Delivery'. But when gradually time passed, people were comfortable with the 'Net-Banking' option and they used it, without any fear. Then the concept of 'E-wallet' came which meant that the payments were made using the mobile phone apps. One such popular application now-a-days is 'Paytm'. In this, you have to make your own account, and store some amount of money from Bank-Account. This is like a wallet where you directly pay your day-to-day transactions using this. This is increasingly becoming common from a small shops to big transactions. Each and every people are aware with this, specially after the demonetisation, where the major concept was going 'cash-less'.

People generally don't see this as an disadvantage, unless and until the application is leaking same details of users, as is not registered or not reputed. So, we can say that 9 out of 10 people are agreed and comfortable excluding its negative element.

Here is the examiner's comment:

> The candidate covers all parts of the task, putting forward many of the advantages of using mobile phone apps to pay for purchases. The reference to disadvantages is rather brief, and the score might be improved by further discussion of these. Ideas and information are presented logically and there is a clear progression throughout the answer. Cohesive devices are used, including some reference [*they used it* | *In this* | *This is like a wallet*] and paragraphing is used adequately. The range of vocabulary is wide enough to show some less common items and collocations [*a major role* | *highlight* | *websites* | *paying online* | *risky* | *transactions* | *leaking* | *registered*] with only occasional errors [*from a small shops* / shop | *specially* / especially | *same* / some | *reputed* / reputable]. The opening paragraph consists entirely of simple sentence structures, but the range broadens later to include more variety. The majority of structures are error-free, although occasional errors occur [*they consider bit risky then* / they considered it to be a bit risky then | *People were not able to believe or put trust* / People were not able to believe or put trust in it | *pay* (for) *your day-to-day transactions* | *Each and every people are aware with this* / Each and every person is aware of this | *an* / *a disadvantage*].

Sample answer sheets

IELTS Listening Answer Sheet

Candidate Name

Candidate No.   Centre No.

Test Date   Day   Month   Year

Listening Listening Listening Listening Listening Listening Listening

	Marker use only			Marker use only
1	1 ✓ ✗	21	21 ✓ ✗
2	2 ✓ ✗	22	22 ✓ ✗
3	3 ✓ ✗	23	23 ✓ ✗
4	4 ✓ ✗	24	24 ✓ ✗
5	5 ✓ ✗	25	25 ✓ ✗
6	6 ✓ ✗	26	26 ✓ ✗
7	7 ✓ ✗	27	27 ✓ ✗
8	8 ✓ ✗	28	28 ✓ ✗
9	9 ✓ ✗	29	29 ✓ ✗
10	10 ✓ ✗	30	30 ✓ ✗
11	11 ✓ ✗	31	31 ✓ ✗
12	12 ✓ ✗	32	32 ✓ ✗
13	13 ✓ ✗	33	33 ✓ ✗
14	14 ✓ ✗	34	34 ✓ ✗
15	15 ✓ ✗	35	35 ✓ ✗
16	16 ✓ ✗	36	36 ✓ ✗
17	17 ✓ ✗	37	37 ✓ ✗
18	18 ✓ ✗	38	38 ✓ ✗
19	19 ✓ ✗	39	39 ✓ ✗
20	20 ✓ ✗	40	40 ✓ ✗

Marker 2 Signature: Marker 1 Signature: Listening Total:

20656

BRITISH COUNCIL **idp** **Cambridge Assessment English**

IELTS Reading Answer Sheet

Candidate Name

Candidate No.

Centre No.

Test Module ☐ Academic ☐ General Training

Test Date Day Month Year

Reading Reading Reading Reading Reading Reading Reading

1	21	
2	22	
3	23	
4	24	
5	25	
6	26	
7	27	
8	28	
9	29	
10	30	
11	31	
12	32	
13	33	
14	34	
15	35	
16	36	
17	37	
18	38	
19	39	
20	40	

Marker use only

Marker 2 Signature:

Marker 1 Signature:

Reading Total:

61788

BRITISH COUNCIL

idp

Cambridge Assessment English

IELTS Writing Answer Sheet - TASK 1

Candidate Name

Candidate No.

Centre No.

Test Module ☐ Academic ☐ General Training

Test Date   Day   Month   Year

If you need more space to write your answer, use an additional sheet and write in the space provided to indicate how many sheets you are using: Sheet ☐ of ☐

Writing Task 1 Writing Task 1 Writing Task 1 Writing Task 1

Do not write below this line

Do not write in this area. Please continue your answer on the other side of this sheet.

23505

BRITISH COUNCIL

idp

Cambridge Assessment English

IELTS Writing Answer Sheet - TASK 2

Candidate Name

Candidate No.

Centre No.

Test Module ☐ Academic ☐ General Training

Test Date

Day | Month | Year

If you need more space to write your answer, use an additional sheet and write in the space provided to indicate how many sheets you are using: Sheet ☐ of ☐

Writing Task 2 Writing Task 2 Writing Task 2 Writing Task 2

Do not write below this line

Do not write in this area. Please continue your answer on the other side of this sheet.

39507

Acknowledgements

The authors and publishers acknowledge the following sources of copyright material and are grateful for the permissions granted. While every effort has been made, it has not always been possible to identify the sources of all the material used, or to trace all copyright holders. If any omissions are brought to our notice, we will be happy to include the appropriate acknowledgements on reprinting and in the next update to the digital edition, as applicable.

Text

Reading – Test 1: Citizens Advice for the adapted text from 'If something you ordered hasn't arrived'. Copyright © Citizens Advice. Reproduced with permission; WorkSafe New Zealand for the adapted text from 'Working on roofs – good practice guidelines', http://construction.worksafe.govt.nz/guides/working-on-roofs/. Copyright © WorkSafe New Zealand; GOV.UK for the adapted text from 'Maternity Allowance', https://www.gov.uk/maternity-allowance. Reproduced under the Open Government Licence v3.0; A&E Television Networks, LLC for the adapted text from History.com Editors 'California Gold Rush' History.com, 29.08.2019. Reproduced with permission. All rights reserved. HISTORY® is a trademark of A&E Television Networks, LLC. All rights reserved; **Test 2:** Sourceable for the adapted text from 'Workplace Health and Safety Considerations for Plumbers' by Emma Bentton, 03.11.2015, https://sourceable.net/workplace-health-and-safety-considerations-for-plumbers/. Reproduced with kind permission; PowWowNow for the adapted text from 'How to manage flexible working with your employees' by Candice Choo. Copyright © 2017 PowWowNow. Reproduced with kind permission; The Guardian for the adapted text from 'How to catch a poacher: *Breaking Bad* and fake eggs' by Jeremy Hance, *The Guardian*, 26.07.2016. Copyright Guardian News & Media Ltd 2019. Reproduced with permission; **Test 3:** Jenny Rogers Coaching Ltd for the adapted text from *Job Interview Success: be your own coach* by Jenny Rogers. Reproduced with kind permission of Jenny Rogers; New Scientist Ltd for the adapted text from 'Lazy fit animals: How some beasts get the gain without the pain' by Richard Lovett, *New Scientist Ltd*, 14.04.2017. Copyright © 2017 New Scientist Ltd. All rights reserved. Distributed by Tribune Content Agency. Reproduced with permission; **Test 4:** The Institution of Engineering and Technology for the adapted text from 'How to make your working day more enjoyable' by Georgina Bloomfield, 29.06.2016. Reproduced with permission; Telegraph Media Group Limited for the text adapted from 'How to get promoted. Fast' by Louisa Symington-Mills, *Telegraph Media Group Limited*, 06.01.2015. Copyright © 2015 Telegraph Media Group Limited. Reproduced with permission; Telegraph Media Group Limited for the text adapted from 'Animals can tell right from wrong' by Richard Gray, *Telegraph Media Group Limited*, 23.05.2009. Copyright © 2015 Telegraph Media Group Limited. Reproduced with permission.

Listening – Harper Collins Publishers Ltd for the adapted text *Consuming passions* by Judith Flanders. Reprinted by permission of HarperCollins Publishers Ltd. Copyright © 2006 Judith Flanders. Reproduced with kind permission; Rogers, Coleridge and White for the adapted text *Consuming passions* by Judith Flanders. Copyright © 2013 Rogers, Coleridge and White; AM Heath & Co. Ltd for the adapted text *Consuming Passions* by Judith Flanders. Copyright © 2008 Judith Flanders. Reproduced by permission of AM Heath & Co. Ltd; Excerpt(s) from *Collapse: How Societies Choose to Fail or Succeed* by Jared Diamond, copyright © 2005 by Jared Diamond. Used by permission of Viking Books, an imprint of Penguin Publishing Group, a division of Penguin Random House LLC. All rights reserved; Seven hundred and ninety-one (791) words in the English language from *Collapse* by Jared Diamond Copyright © Jared Diamond, 2005, 2011.

Illustration

Illustrations commissioned by Cambridge Assessment.

Audio

Audio production by Real Deal Productions and dsound recording.

Typesetting

Typeset by QBS Learning.

URLs

The publisher has used its best endeavours to ensure that the URLs for external websites referred to in this book are correct and active at the time of going to press. However, the publisher has no responsibility for the websites and can make no guarantee that a site will remain live or that the content is or will remain appropriate.

Practice
Makes Perfect

Get more out of Authentic Practice Tests

Lesson Plans

Teacher Tips

Extra Support

- Get Tips and Tricks to use in your classroom
- Download complete lesson plans for practice test questions
- Explore the extra support, training and technology available for your exam

Find out more at
practicemakesperfect.cambridge.org

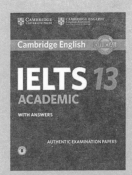

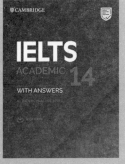

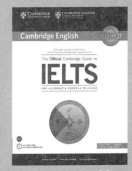